Deadly!

Deadly!

Confronting the 7 deadly sins

STEVE DUPLESSIE

ANAPAUO PRESS, ATTLEBORO, MA
2012

Deadly: Confronting the 7 deadly sins
with Study Guide

DuPlessie, J. Stephen, 1952-

© 2012, 2014 and 2018 by Steve DuPlessie. All rights reserved.

Published by Anapauo Press
47 Patterson Street, Attleboro, Massachusetts

First edition – October, 2012
Second edition – October, 2014

ISBN 978-0615657264

Printed in the United States of America

Cover design by Erika Houghton
Page layout design by Steve DuPlessie
Author photo by Matt DuPlessie
Front cover photo by iStockphoto.com

Unless otherwise noted, all Scriptures are taken from
THE HOLY BIBLE, NEW INTERNATIONAL VERSION®, NIV®
Copyright © 1973, 1978, 1984, 2011 by Biblica, Inc.™
Used by permission. All rights reserved worldwide.

This book is dedicated to Deb
and to our family — Matt & Beth,
Meegan & Mike, Maura & Jon,
and their growing tribe of
kids — who constantly show me
grace and make me very proud.

Contents

Introduction   Confronting the 7 deadly sins   IX

Chapter 1   Pride goes before the...   1

Chapter 2   Greedy! Greedy! Greedy!   13

Chapter 3   I want that!   27

Chapter 4   Ohhhh!   38

Chapter 5   Whatever   55

Chapter 6   Urrrgh!   72

Chapter 7   Supersized   92

Chapter 8   P-E-G-L-A-G-S   105

Appendix   The Navigators Topical   113
Memory System

Introduction

For a number of years Bob Gilbert has been part of the Good News Bible Chapel (GNBC) family in Attleboro, Massachusetts where I serve as an elder and the staff Teaching Pastor. Bob frequently refers in conversations to The Seven Deadly Sins, a favorite topic of his. To be honest, I've never really paid much attention to this ancient, classic list, being preoccupied instead with my own current list of persistent vices.

A little history...

But over time Bob's comments intrigued me. What are The Seven Deadly Sins? Where did this particular list come from since there are obviously a lot more than seven sins? And all of them are deadly. I soon discovered that a 4th century Roman Catholic monk, Evagrius Ponticus, listed eight evil thoughts in Greek: gastrimargia (gluttony), porneia (fornication), philargyria (avarice), hyperēphania (hubris), lypē (sadness at another's good fortune), orgē (wrath), kenodoxia (boasting), and akēdia (acedia or dejection).

These were later translated from the Greek—largely through the writings of a Scythian monk, the 5th century Dessert Father, John Cassian—into the Latin of Western

Christianity as gluttony, lust, greed, pride, sorrow, wrath, vainglory and sloth. And they come down to us today as a list, reduced by Pope Gregory I in the 6th century, from eight to seven vices: gluttony, lust, greed, pride, envy, anger and sloth.

Ancient but still present...

Okay, so the list is ancient. But they are all still very much with us today. And they are all still very deadly. While some like gluttony and anger can be physically deadly, all these and more are spiritually deadly in that all sin separates us from God (Isaiah 59:2) and earns us the full weight of his wrath (Romans 1:18; 2:5; Ephesians 5:6) and finally a death penalty (Romans 5:12; 6:23; Ephesians 2:1, 2).

Fortunately for us, the good news is that Christ has already taken on himself all of his Father's hot, holy wrath (1 Thessalonians 5:9, 10; 1 Peter 2:24) and fully paid the penalty on the cross that our sin deserves (Hebrews 9:15; 1 Peter 3:18). Praise God!

But we still wrestle—actually, sometimes we don't fight very hard—with the temptations to sin. I know I do. And this old list of The Seven Deadly Sins is still very much with us today. Some like Lust are amplified and spread far and wide by our advances in technology. Some like Pride and even Greed are valued and promoted as character strengths in our narcissistic and materialistic culture. And others like Envy and Gluttony are the foundation of corporate marketing plans worldwide. The headlines of newspapers and the 6 o'clock news are filled with stories of Anger turned violent. And even Sloth is all around us, not only in the ubiquitous litter that lines our streets and highways, but in the smaller, unseen habits (or the lack thereof) of our private lives.

So they are all here. And like all sins they are still deadly. And they are still confronted directly—and helpfully—by the teaching of Jesus. Each of these vices has a corresponding virtue that needs to be cultivated, fed, encouraged, valued. And Jesus is the prime example of the virtues. They are worth exploring together.

I encourage you to have your bible in hand with a pen as you read this book. It is taken, as might become obvious, directly from a series of seven sermons I gave at GNBC in the spring of 2012. I have edited them a little to minimize local references. But the flavor of the sermons is still here. And having your bible open as you read this book—taking the time to look up the key verses, underlining those verses, and making notes in the margins of your bible—it will all help to make this not just another book you've read, and not just another study to do, but rather I pray it is a direct and hard confrontation of The Seven Deadly Sins, a personal discovery of their corresponding virtues, and an opportunity for the Word of God to shine a bright light of self-examination on you that can lead to God-exalting liberty and victory in your life.

Steve DuPlessie
Attleboro, Massachusetts
September, 2012

CHAPTER 1

Pride goes before the...

Pride goes before destruction,
a haughty spirit before a fall.
- Proverbs 16:18

L ike most of us, I'm usually clueless that pride is an issue for me. We get so close to something—get so comfortable with an attitude, so tight with a way of thinking—that we can't even see what is pretty obvious to everyone else around us. In fact, we think we're right, we're justified, we're perfectly within our rights to indulge the pride that usually shows up in selfishness, self-absorption, or ambition. It shows up in a whole pile of very different and not-so-obvious ways.

For example, I'm thinking of TV's House, MD who doesn't seem to care what he says or who he offends. Or any of a long list of A-game athletes, maybe like Metta World Peace (formerly Ron Artest, Jr.), the NBA player who gives out free concussions on the basketball court, and seems totally clueless to his arrogance.

So, I don't consider myself proud, but if I'm pretty sure that I'm usually the smartest person in the room, or that I know more about the best solution to your financial circumstances, or your health care, or your work situation, or you name it, than you do. Um ... that's my pride.

Or maybe I think it's pretty obvious that immigrants are not the same as me—in spite of being made in the image of God, just like me, and wrestling with the same brokenness of sin that I wrestle with every day.

Or, changing the scene for a moment, maybe I think that I deserve some new clothes, or deserve some time alone, or deserve a night out, because, well, *I deserve it.*

Or, changing the scene again, maybe I'm pretty focused on how I look, what I wear (always the latest, or coolest, or just new or alternatively, I work really hard to be different), maybe I obsess about my hair (or even that my hair was so thin and so white that maybe I would look younger bald!). Or, maybe my self-image and self-worth and identity are tied directly to external things like my cool car, or my big house, or my degree, or my title, or my job, or...

Or, changing scenes yet again, maybe I can't admit to my wife (or even myself) that she's right and I'm wrong this time. So my false picture of myself means there are some things that we can't even talk about in our marriage—there is this huge *"Don't go there!"* zone in our relationship. And that might even extend to work—where I can't admit to anyone that I'm wrong, or that I don't know what to do next, or that I can't ask for help.

And maybe my pride is actually a deep sense of class or race or identity, like Mr. Darcy in *Pride and Prejudice*: I'm better than the people around me because I'm a responsible Republican (or a big-hearted Democrat), I'm a guy, or I'm white, or I'm from an ancient and superior culture, or I'm better educated, or whatever.

You get the point. Pride is ubiquitous and insidious, deeper and more complex than just bragging about *whatever.* And here's the thing. Pride is not just un-cool and socially awkward; pride is not just arrogant or offensive. Pride is not just a marriage buster or career breaker. Pride, at its core, comes from a deep and untrue picture of yourself. And to deal with pride, you need to deal with truth.

Big Truth #1

Big truth #1 is you and I are created by God (Psalm 139:13, 14; Isaiah 42:5; 43:7; Romans 9:20; Psalm 119:73) and you are made in the image of God[1] (Genesis 1:26, 27, see Isaiah 45:9). You are of such personal value that God knows you personally by name (John 10:27. See also Isaiah 43:1; John 10:1-3, 14, 15; 2 Timothy 2:19), and you are so deeply loved by God (John 3:16; Romans 5:8; Ephesians 2:4, 5; 1 John 4:10) that he sent his one and only Son to die to redeem you (Romans 5:6-8; Ephesians 1:7). God has

---

[1] I understand the *Imago Dei* (Latin for Image of God) like this: I don't think my late miserable cat, PeeWee, in her quiet thoughtful moments, ever managed to contemplate God. But we humans are special spiritual beings who can conceive of the concept of God and can desire to know God. And because we are made in his image we can pursue love, grace, mercy, justice...just some of the many attributes of God—making us unique in all of earth's creation.

chosen you (Ephesians 1:4; 2 Thessalonians 2:13), making you his own choice possession (Ephesians 1:14). If you believe in Jesus you are adopted by God as his own dear child (John 1:12; Romans 8:16; Ephesians 1:5; 1 John 3:1) and as his child, you are now an heir of all the promises of the kingdom of God (1 Peter 1:3, 4; Acts 20:32; Galatians 3:29; 4:7; Ephesians 3:6)! And, on top of all that, you are God's proudly designed master-piece, his "workman-ship" (Ephesians 2:10). So you have great, fantastic, inestim-able, intrinsic, inerasable, eternal worth. And your worth is not found in what you wear or what you do or what you own but who you are in the sight of God—his created, loved, chosen, redeemed, forgiven, adopted child! Wow! That's Big Truth #1.

> "I praise you because I am fearfully and wonderfully made; Your works are wonderful, I know that full well."
>
> - Psalm 139:14

Take a moment and let that very powerful and very personal truth sink in. If you have been finding your identity and worth in something you do—maybe a skill in sports or a talent like music or art, a degree from a prestigious school or a career path filled with success and money, or maybe your self-worth is all about where you live, your culture or your social class, or maybe if you identify yourself through your family, your children and grandchildren—if your worth is tied to some*thing*, anything other than the fact that you are made in the image of God who loves you and sent his one and only Son to die for you—then you are missing out on a deep and powerful truth that has lasting value when your sports skills fade, your career ends, your money is gone or your family disappoints you.

Then again, if your identity is all tied to something that has happened in your life—maybe you are a child of divorced parents or an orphan. Maybe you are from a class or race that has been marginalized or victimized for generations. Maybe you are the victim of abuse or a great personal tragedy like a disabling disease or condition, or a dreadful accident, or in a great loss. If your identity is tied up in these and so many other sad circumstances of life, you are missing out on your identity as one deeply loved by God, as one personally known by God, as a chosen, adopted child of God—an identity that is so much deeper than the circumstances of your life. Take a few moments and soak in that life-altering, mind-changing truth.

Big Truth #2

On the other hand, it's *also* true that you and I are broken sinners who are separated far from God (Isaiah 53:6; 59:2), totally lost and without any hope (Ephesians 2:12), on the broad road to hell (Matthew 7:13) and desperately in need of a savior who can cover over our sin (1 John 4:10). We need a savior who can reintroduce us to God in a new relationship (John 3:3; 1 Peter 3:18), not based on our foolish and failed attempts to be good (Isaiah 64:6; Titus

3:5), but based solely on the goodness of our savior (1 Peter 2:24) and God's amazing grace alone (Ephesians 2:8, 9). Our desperate brokenness is Big Truth #2.

And it's the failure to recognize and hold this Big Truth #2 in balance with Big Truth #1 that leads to pride. To forget that I am made in the image of God, known by God and deeply loved by God but broken—loved but broken just like everyone else all around me, no matter how they look on the outside.[2]

And this pride? It stinks to God. There's no other way to say it. Consider these clear scriptures: Proverbs 16:5, "The LORD detests all the proud of heart. Be sure of this: They will not go unpunished." Psalm 31:23, "The LORD preserves the faithful, but the proud he pays back in full." Psalm 101:5, "Whoever has haughty eyes and a proud heart, him will God not endure."

What's the problem? Pride of any sort is first an insult to God, because pride puts us, exalts you and me, above God. After all, pride is first and foremost all about me, and God doesn't figure there anywhere, except as God might serve me and my good or my goals. Second, pride gets in the way of an honest, open-eyed picture of ourselves (the picture that most everyone else around us has of us!) and gets in the way of living authentically and humbly with each other as a disciple, a follower of Jesus.

---

[2] It is always a mistake to compare my insides with everyone else's outside.

Is there an answer?

So what's the answer for someone who genuinely wants to be real in their claim to be a Christian, a follower of Jesus? Well, the first step is to call sin for what it is, sin. My obsession with myself—encouraged by the culture that says "Pay attention to #1. Take care of yourself first, after all, you deserve it!"—my obsession with myself is not a character flaw, it's not a personality weakness. God calls it sin. And all sin—my sin, your sin—stinks to God. If I want to grow deeper in my spiritual life, if I want to be closer to God, if I want to be genuine in my worship, if I want to be real in my public life as a follower of Jesus, then first I need to admit to myself that sin is sin. To be honest about sin is to hate sin just as God hates it.

Listen, I'm afraid that too often I excuse my sin—that's *just the way I am*! Or I minimize my sin—it's not really all *that* bad! No. To admit your sin is to begin to hate your sin as much as God hates your sin. And until you hate your sin as much as God does and until you want to run from it—run from it to God for forgiveness and grace—until then, you don't see your sin yet as God does.

So first, I need to admit my sin to myself, name it. Second, I need to admit it to God—confess it—as sin. Listen, it's not like God doesn't know anything about it until I confess my sin; no, actually it's that God is waiting for me to admit to myself and agree with him that what I'm thinking and doing is sin that offends his brilliant, pure and spotless holiness.

Fortunately, God promises that "If we confess our sins, God is faithful and just to forgive us our sins and purify us from all unrighteousness"(1 john 1:8,9). We don't usually take time to confess our sins—though we surely could and should more often because confession is good for the soul. Confession admits our total dependence on God for his gifts to us of his love and mercy and grace. If confession is not part of your daily prayer life—"Forgive us our sins as we forgive those who sin against us..."—if confession is not part of your daily spiritual disciplines, you need to make an adjustment and confess your sin to God daily, seeking his forgiveness, claiming his promise to forgive all your sin for Jesus' sake.

First, admit your sin to yourself; name it. Second, admit your sin to God; confess it. Third, replace it. Repent, that is, turn from your sin and replace it ... with virtue. We'll talk more about this in the next chapters, but for our discussion here, replace the sin of pride with the virtue of humility.

That is a totally foreign concept in our culture! Humility! Are you kidding me? You want me to choose to be humble? One of the things that drove the sportswriters crazy in the fall of 2011 was the humility of the Denver Broncos' quarterback, Tim Tebow. He refused to take credit for leading the Broncos to the playoffs and instead he gave the credit to the team. And then early in 2012, on the heels of "Tebowing," came "Linsannity" with Jeremy Lin, the NY Nicks point guard whose rise from an end-of-the-bench nobody to superstar happened in just a few weeks. And Lin refused to take personal credit for pulling the Nicks out of their slump. Both Tebow and Lin are outspoken but humble Christians, and both are totally counter cultural. Counter cultural and totally radical in following Jesus in humility.

Too often we misunder-stand humility. Listen, humility is not putting yourself down. Humility is not denying your strengths, your skills, your abilities. C.S. Lewis wrote "Humility is not thinking less of yourself; humility is thinking of yourself less."[3] Let me repeat that sentence because it is the key concept of this chapter and is so totally countercultural, so totally radical, and so totally biblical: "Humility is not thinking less of yourself; humility is thinking of yourself less."

Humility is not thinking less of yourself; humility is thinking of yourself less.

Jesus said. "If anyone wants to be first, he must be the very last, and the servant of all." Talk about counter-cultural! Talk about radical! The apostle Paul wrote "Live in harmony with one another. Do not be proud, but be willing to associate with people of low position" (Romans 12:16). What, hang out with the people of low position in society, the least, the lowly, the meek the poor? What, sell my comfortable house in the

---

[33] This great quote is attributed variously to C. S. Lewis, Watchman Nee, and even Mohandas Gandhi, Rick Warren and Tim Keller. I can't verify who said it first. But it has been repeated many times with little effort at clarifying who should be given initial credit. That's kind of strange for a quote about humility, don't you think?

suburbs and move to an apartment in the inner city to be close to my neighbors, "the least of these" like Dave and Danielle Ambrose did in Hartford, Connecticut? Really?

Our example of choosing humility over pride or hubris is Jesus. Look, it's always all about Jesus. In this particular case, Jesus, the most powerful man in the room, is the one who washed the feet of his own students (John 13:2-16). Turn in your bible with me to the small letter by the apostle Paul to the Christ-followers in Philippi; Philippians, chapter 2, verse 1. Paul writes...

"If you have any encouragement from being united with Christ, if any comfort from his love, if any fellowship with the Spirit, if any tenderness and compassion, then make my joy complete by being like-minded, having the same love, being one in spirit and purpose. Do nothing out of selfish ambition or vain conceit, but in humility consider others better than yourselves. Each of you should look not only to your own interests, but also to the interests of others.

> **Q**
> **What do you do when you are the most powerful person in the room?**
>
> What do you do when you are the highest level leader at the meeting, the smartest on taskforce, the best player on the team? How does a follower of Jesus with real skills and abilities act in situations like that? Jesus said, "Wash their feet." Instead of thinking of yourself, think about what will build others up, what would benefit those around you. (See Ephesians 4:29)

"Your attitude should be the same as that of Christ Jesus: Who, being in very nature God, did not consider equality with God something to be grasped (or held onto), but made himself nothing, taking the very nature of a servant, being made in human likeness. And being found in appearance as a man, he humbled himself and became obedient to death—even death on a cross! Therefore God exalted him to the highest place and gave him the name that is above every name, that at the name of Jesus every knee should bow, in heaven and on earth and under the earth, and every tongue confess that Jesus Christ is Lord, to the glory of God the Father."

Your example, your model for humility, for thinking of others more and yourself less, is Jesus.

I was trying to think of something that would be a good visual, a powerful object lesson that I could use to nail the point of what we're talking about here. And actually, Jesus himself already gave us the most powerful but simple object lesson to make the point. It's right on the Communion Table in the loaf of bread that is a symbol of his own physical body that was given at great personal sacrifice for us (Luke 19:22) and the wine or juice that is a symbol of the blood of the sinless, spotless Son of God that was poured out so that we can be forgiven (Romans 5:9; see Hebrews 9:22; 10:19, 20) and washed clean (1 John 1:7) of all our sin. Talk about humility!

Digging deeper...

1. "Big Truth #1 is you and I are created by God and you are made in the image of God" (See Gen 1:26, 27). What about that statement impacts you the most? Why?

2. Big Truth #2 says "You and I are broken sinners who are separated far from God (Isaiah 53:6; 59:2), totally lost and without any hope (Ephesians 2:12), on the broad road to hell (Matthew 7:13) and desperately in need a savior who can cover over our sin (1 John 4:10)." How do you balance "made in the image of God" with "broken, lost and hopeless?"

3. If "Humility is not thinking less of yourself; it is thinking of yourself less," what changes do you have to make to deal with pride in your life?

CHAPTER 2

Greedy! Greedy! Greedy!

The love of money is a root of all kinds of evil.
Some people, eager for money, have wandered from the faith
and pierced themselves with many griefs
- 1 Timothy 6:10

We're looking at the classic list of the seven deadly sins. The last chapter launched the topic by looking at pride—and I think I did an excellent job! ☺ And while looking at pride we also explored the corresponding virtue of humility. Remember, we said that humility is not thinking less of yourself; humility is thinking of yourself less. We're in this chapter to look at greed.

Do you remember the classic *"Greed is good!"* speech by Michael Douglas playing the fabulously successful but crooked stockbroker, Gordon Gekko, in the 1987 film *Wall Street*. In the audience for that speech is the young Martin Sheen playing Ben Fox, a stockbroker who decides he wants to be just like Gekko. The movie ends with both Gekko and Ben going to prison for illegal insider trading, but only after Ben finally gets a conscience and does right thing to bring Gekko down.

And the ironic thing is that the movie—and that quote, "Greed is good"—instead of making the obvious moral lesson that greed is bad, actually inspired thousands of Gekko wannabes to go into Wall Street and banking careers. And they made tons of money. And 20 years later they brought us the 2008 financial collapse that wrecked America, threw millions into foreclosure and unemployment, and set America's economy back for what looks like the better part of a decade. I know that there were a lot of factors in the collapse— inflated housing prices, people getting mortgages who couldn't pay the bill, reinsurance schemes gone wild, all that stuff. But the economy collapsed, and greed survives.

> **Q**
>
> *For a sincere follower of Jesus, what's the answer to the income gap? How should I think and act about money? Is getting more money bad? Should I feel guilty?*

And then came the Occupy Movement—as much as I despise their lawless, anarchist tactics, they do accurately point out with the voice of an OT prophet that first, there is a growing gap between the haves and have-nots, and second, economic injustice seems to be just a speed bump to be overcome by the greedy. So the question I want to explore here for a few minutes with you is this: For a sincere follower of Jesus, what's the answer to the income gap? How should I think and act about money? Is getting more money bad for someone who wants to follow Jesus? Should I feel guilty if I earn more money than someone else as some suggest? Is getting a good, solid education so I can get a good, solid job actually a bad thing? Or is it a good thing? Should I give up trying to earn more money, hey, should I give my job to someone who doesn't have a job right now? Is making a lot of money immoral? What should I be thinking about money as a disciple of Jesus?

Well, Jesus talked about money. Maybe that's because money was as important in Jesus' day as it is now. Maybe Jesus talked a lot about money because money was as much a problem then as it is now. Maybe Jesus talked so much about money because greed was as deadly a sin back then as it still is now.

As Christians, we're "People of the book." That's where we go for answers to the big questions of life. So, turn in your bible with me to the first gospel, Matthew, the first of the four gospels or biographies of the life and ministry of Jesus, Matthew, chapter 19. Look down at verse 16 with me...

"Now a man came up to Jesus and asked, 'Teacher, what good thing must I do to get eternal life?' 'Why do you ask me about what is good?' Jesus replied. 'There is only One who is good. If you want to enter life, obey the commandments.'

Verse 18: "'Which ones?' the man inquired. Jesus replied, 'Do not murder, do not commit adultery, do not steal, do not give false testimony, honor your father and mother,' and 'love your neighbor as yourself.'"

Verse 20: "'All these I have kept,' the young man said. 'What do I still lack?' Jesus answered, 'If you want to be perfect, go, sell your possessions and give to the poor, and you will have treasure in heaven. Then come, follow me.'

"When the young man heard this, he went away sad, because he had great wealth. Then Jesus said to his disciples, 'I tell you the truth, it is hard for a rich man to enter the kingdom of heaven. Again I tell you, it is easier for a camel to go through the eye of a needle than for a rich man to enter the kingdom of God.' When the disciples heard this, they were greatly astonished and asked, 'Who then can be saved?' Jesus looked at them and said, 'With man this is impossible, but with God all things are possible.'"

Let's unpack that story for a few minutes together. Look back at verse 16 with me. Now a man came up to Jesus and asked, "Teacher, what good thing must I do to get eternal life?" The man seems to be sincere. After all, he's the one who sought out Jesus and asked the question, "What good thing must I do to get eternal life?" So he's sincere, but somewhat misguided. He's on the same religious treadmill as millions of sincere, devout people. He knows that there is something bigger, something beyond this life. And he wants eternal life, life beyond this life on earth, but he thinks he has to do something good to earn it.

He thinks if he's good enough, he'll earn, he'll merit, hey, he'll *deserve* eternal life! God will owe it to him! If he does all the right, all the good things then God is on the hook, right?

(Listen, just a short rabbit trail here: There are tons of TV preachers today who want you to think that God wants you to be rich, that being rich is the sign of God's blessing. As if somehow being saved from the penalty of sin and adopted into the eternal family of God is not blessing enough. They want you to think that God owes you riches if you prime the pump with your offering. God is on the hook to give you wealth if you just ... fill in the blank. I don't see it. Jesus, who was homeless, who had just a shirt for his only possession in the world when he died, he wants you to be rich? Really? Never. He never promised it.)

Look at verse 17: "Why do you ask me about what is good?" Jesus replied. "There is only One who is good. If you want to enter life, obey the commandments." "Which ones?" the man inquired. Jesus replied, "'Do not murder, do not commit adultery, do not steal, do not give false testimony, honor your father and mother,' and 'love your neighbor as yourself.'" Jesus is repeating what? Of course, he's restating five of the Ten Commandments. The Ten Commandments that show us what God's standard of goodness looks like. The first four of the ten are about our relationship with God. The last six of the ten are about our relationship with each other.

Then the man replied "'All these I have kept,' the young man said." Really? "'What do I still lack?' Jesus answered him, 'If you want to be perfect, go, sell your possessions and give to the poor, and you will have treasure in heaven. Then come, follow me.'" Follow me into homelessness, follow me into traveling around the countryside, village to village, living on whatever friends give me, essentially, living with nothing. "When the young man heard this, he went away sad, because he had great wealth."

What was the problem here? I mean, the man already said that he kept all the commandments, all Ten of them. Never messed up. Never missed one. So that means, he's perfect. Sinless. Blameless. So what's the problem?

> *Jesus—who was homeless, who had just a shirt for his sole possession when he died—wants you to be rich. Really?*

Well, apparently the young man was pretty rich and he didn't want to give up his riches. Somehow he wanted to do good as long as it didn't cost him much. He wanted to earn heaven, without having to pay lot! He wanted to be close to God, but he didn't want to give up his money. So, I guess you could say that his money was more precious, more important to him than God. And when anything is more precious to us, more important to us—when we love something more than we love God—that's idolatry. Which messes with the first of the Ten Commandments, "You will have no other gods before me."

So, instead of keeping all Ten Commandments like he thought, this guy already failed at number one! He didn't want to give up his riches here on earth, and he didn't trust the promise Jesus made that he would have great treasure waiting for him in heaven. He loved his money more than he loved God. He trusted his money more than he trusted Jesus.

Jesus continued, "I tell you the truth, it is hard for a rich man to enter the kingdom of heaven. Again I tell you, it is easier for a camel to go through the eye of a needle than for a rich man to enter the kingdom of God." Why do you think it's so hard for a rich person to enter the kingdom of heaven? Sure. It's way too easy to love riches more than loving God. And when we love something more than we love God, that's called idolatry. This man's money had become his idol; something that replaced God in his affections. Money—and all the things money can buy—directly competes with God for our love, our affection, and our service.

What seems to be the problem here?

So let me ask again, what was the problem here? Is the problem that the man had a lot of money? Actually no, the money itself was not really the problem. It was the love of money that was the problem. The Apostle Paul revisited this when he wrote a letter to his young protégée, Timothy, and said "The love of money is a root of all kinds of evil. Some people, eager for money, have wandered from the faith and pierced themselves with many griefs" (1 Timothy 6:10).

Listen, money isn't the problem. Love of money, greed, is the problem. And you don't have to be rich to love money. I've met many people, some of pretty modest income, some who are downright broke and poor, who still l-o-v-e money and the stuff money buys. Love of money is the problem. Holding on tightly to money is the problem. Not being content with what you have is the problem. Wanting money and stuff more than you want God is the problem. Trusting money more than you trust God is the problem. Trusting money to make you happy is the problem—just ask the winners of the Lottery. Trusting money to protect you, to provide for you; trusting money more than you trust God is the problem.

Jesus taught about money because Jesus knows that money—and money-related stuff like gambling and lotteries, like investments and retirement funds, like all the nice stuff that money can buy—money presents opportunities for Satan to tempt us to love stuff more than we love God. Money presents opportunities for Satan to tempt us to trust money and not trust the Lord. In fact, our attitude and our decisions regarding money are an accurate barometer of our discipleship relationship with Jesus. Money, and money-related circumstances, present opportunities for the Lord to test our trust and faith, and for us to test the Lord's trustworthiness and faithfulness.

So, if greed is not good, if greed is bad, than what is the virtue that has to replace greed? Here it is: charity. Turn a few pages toward the back of your bible from Matthew 19, turn to Ephesians—the short letter by the apostle Paul to the Christ-followers in Ephesus—Ephesians, find chapter 4, look down at verse 17. The apostle Paul writes...

"So I tell you this, and insist on it in the Lord, that you must no longer live as the Gentiles do, (Who are the Gentiles? It's just a term Paul is using for anyone who is not following Jesus; Gentiles - Greeks, Romans, pagans, anyone) you must no longer live as the Gentiles do in the futility of their thinking. They are darkened in their understanding and separated from the life of God because of the ignorance that is in them due to the hardening of their hearts. Having lost all sensitivity, they have given themselves over to sensuality so as to indulge in every kind of impurity, with a continual lust for more. (Sound familiar?)

"You, however, did not come to know Christ that way. Surely you heard of him and were taught in him in accordance with the truth that is in Jesus. You were taught, with regard to your former way of life, to put off your old self, which is being corrupted by its deceitful desires; to be made new in the attitude of your minds; and to put on the new self, created to be like God in true righteousness and holiness."

The Put-Off/Put-On Principle...
What is this? This is the Put-Off/Put-On Principle. Put off the old self: the old way of living, the old BC (Before Christ)

way of thinking; and instead replace it, put on the new self, the Christ-following self, the Disciple-of-Jesus self, the radical-not-conforming-to-culture self. Do not be conformed to the thinking of the world around you but be transformed by the renewing of your mind. Put-Off and Put-On.

So now Paul provides a few examples of what Put-Off/Put-On looks like. Verse 25: "Therefore each of you must put off falsehood (telling lies) and instead speak truthfully to his neighbor, for we are all members of one body." Stop being a liar and begin telling the truth. What's wrong with lying? No one can trust you! No one knows what to believe from you if you are a liar! Put off falsehood and instead put on speaking truthfully.

Verse 26: "In your anger do not sin. Do not let the sun go down while you are still angry, and do not give the devil a foothold." Now notice verse 28 for our point about greed, "He who has been stealing must steal no longer, but must work, doing something useful with his own hands, that he may have something to share with those in need."

Here's the point for us. We need to replace greed—the root that is underneath stealing and another way of saying "loving money"—we need to replace greed with first, hard work. There's nothing wrong with hard work. God designed you, he gave you abilities and strengths so that you can work hard. In fact, in another letter the apostle Paul says "If you don't work, you shouldn't eat!" (2 Thessalonians 3:10). Harsh language! Paul is saying, be responsible for yourself! Don't mooch off others. Get the education you need to get a job and work hard to take care of yourself and your family. No excuses!

But notice the last part of verse 28: "He who has been stealing must steal no longer, but must work, doing something useful with his own hands so..." Why? ... so he can have a bigger house? Another car? More toys? "He who has been stealing must steal no longer, but must work, doing something useful with his own hands so that so that he may have something to share with those in need." The corresponding virtue is charity. Generosity. Giving instead of taking.

> **Generosity:**
>
> *God doesn't give you money to bless you; God gives you money so you can bless others.*

As I write this I am just finishing a course on the history of the early church. Even though the Greek and Roman idol worshippers of the first three centuries of the church didn't like the new Christianity that was spreading all over the Roman empire, they had to admit that the Christians took care of the poor and the widows among them—and even the poor and the widows who were not Christians. Julian, the last of the Roman emperors, tried desperately to revive paganism; he built new temples and spruced up the old ones, but Christianity was spreading faster than he could compete with. In the midst of this, Julian wrote to a friend, a pagan priest: "Nothing has contributed to the progress of the superstition of these

Christians as their charity to strangers, the impious[4] Galileans provide not only for their own poor but for ours as well!" The early Christians were kind and promiscuous with their charity. Prodigal. Generous. Extravagant. Wouldn't it be cool if Christians in the world today were known for the same thing!

And again, our example, our model for Christian charity, for outrageous, prodigal, extravagant generosity is Jesus. Paul writes, "For you know the grace of our Lord Jesus Christ, that though he was rich, yet for your sakes he became poor, so that you through his poverty might become rich" (2 Corinthians 8:9). Jesus gave away all the prerogatives, all the privileges, all the glories of heaven, to condescend, to cloak his deity with a veil of flesh in the incarnation,[5] and finally

> *"Nothing has contributed to the progress of the superstition of these Christians as their charity to strangers, the impious Galileans provide not only for their own poor but for ours as well!"*
>
> Julian, the last of the Roman Emperors

---

[4] Followers of Jesus were considered impious atheists because they refused to bow down to the pantheon of pagan gods.

[5] Speaking of Jesus, the French reformer John Calvin wrote in his commentary on Philippians chapter 2, "In order to exhort us to submission by his example, he shows that when as God he might have displayed to the world the brightness of His glory, he gave up his right, a voluntary emptying of himself; that he assumed the form of a servant, and contented with that humble condition, suffered his divinity to be concealed

to take on himself all the guilt and shame of your sin and mine (1 Peter 2:24) so that you can be forgiven, you can be justified, made new in God's sight, you can be given all the goodness, the holiness, the righteous-ness of Jesus (2nd Corinthians 5:21), and you can be adopted into God's family and made an heir of his kingdom—so that you, through his poverty, might become rich.

Listen, the first century Christians turned their world upside down by preaching of the good news of God's extravagant mercy, his generous grace through the sacrificial death and resurrection of Jesus, a message that they demonstrated with their own practical, outrageous, prodigal, extravagant generosity. God didn't give them money to bless them; he gave them money so that they could bless others.

So, what would it look like if you saw the money God has given you as a tool to bless others? What would it look like if your church was known in the community as the church that blesses the poor? Take a moment and reflect on what God is saying to you about greed and charity in your life, in your home and your church.

---

under a veil of flesh (*cf.* Hebrews 10:19, 20)." *Institutes of the Christian Religion,* Book 2, Chapter 13, pt. 2.

Digging deeper...

1. How is the Prosperity gospel—with it's tempting but false message that Jesus wants you to be rich—inconstant with the life of Jesus himself? Can you identify a Bible verse that speaks to how Jesus wants you to view money?

2. Steve wrote that we need to replace greed with hard work and generosity. Read 1 Timothy 6:10 and 2 Thessalonians 3:10 and summarize your thoughts here.

3. Read 2 Corinthians 8:9 and Philippians 2:5-11. How is the example of Jesus the model for you in generosity?

4. Think about your own philosophy of a biblical understanding of money. Write it out on a separate piece of paper.

CHAPTER 3

I want that!

A tranquil heart gives life to the flesh,
but envy makes the bones rot.
- Proverbs 14:30

You shall not covet your neighbor's house;
you shall not covet your neighbor's wife, or his male
servant, or his female servant, or his ox, or his donkey,
or anything that is your neighbor's.
- Exodus 20:17

Resentment kills a fool,
and envy slays the simple.
- Job 5:2

So you are still reading. Good. I haven't scared you away yet by talking about pride or greed. We're looking at the classic list of The Seven Deadly Sins. In the first chapter we talked about pride and said that the antithesis of pride

27

is humility. And humility is not thinking less of yourself but thinking of yourself less. Chapter two discussed greed and we saw that the corresponding virtue is charity or outrageous, prodigal, extravagant generosity. And we said God doesn't give you money to bless you; God gives you money to bless others.

And now we are talking about the first cousin of greed, a vice called envy. What's envy? One dictionary says "Envy is a feeling of discontented or resentful longing aroused by someone else's possessions, qualities, or luck." Good old Merriam-Webster's Dictionary says that "Envy is painful or resentful awareness of an advantage enjoyed by another, joined with a desire to possess the same advantage."

Ever been there? Ever had a feeling of "discontented or resentful longing" aroused by someone else's possessions, or maybe even their qualities? Ever had "painful or resentful awareness of an advantage enjoyed by another, joined with a desire to possess the same advantage?"

I remember when I was a kid, envying my buddy Dennis who had a little beagle; that happy little dog was always waiting in the yard, tail wagging, jumping up and down, waiting for Dennis when we got out of elementary school every day. I thought I wanted a dog like that, waiting for me to come home, ready to play, every day.

And to be honest, more than once I've kinda lusted after a new, sleeker, lightweight fiberglass kayak like the one that my friend Jim has instead of my chubby, roto-molded poly boat. Okay, so that is the short list of my envy issues. And you know what is common to my envy stuff;

did you see what was common in those two definitions? Discontentment and resentful longing.

We live in a culture of discontentment. I worked in advertising and marketing for 25 years and one of the goals of advertising is to create discontentment; discontentment with what you have so that you simply have go out and buy this new, new thing. The old phone doesn't have the apps, the speed, the screen that the new iPhone has. The old car doesn't have the cool video and auto-parking and whatever else that a new car has. The old ... you name it. The old husband doesn't have the trim body, the funny laugh, the income, of the guy at the health club. The old wife doesn't have the trim body, the funny laugh, the cute smile of the girl at the health club...

And discontentment breeds resentful longing. Don't I deserve to be happy too? Don't I deserve a new... you fill in the blank: a new phone or a new TV or a bigger office or a better parking spot or ... What is it for you? "Don't I deserve a wife who isn't exhausted all the time? I wish I had Burt's wife." "Don't I deserve a husband more like my office manager who pays more attention to me than he does to sports?"

More than just longing for something new and different, faster and better, discontentment breeds resentful longing: "It's not fair that the 1% has more money than the 99%, so they should give their money to me." "It's not fair that she has ... and I don't." "It's not fair that he has ... and I don't." Envy that smolders underneath the surface, like a hot coal buried in the ash of the fireplace.

So what is going on with envy? I've got a couple of thoughts. First, my envy means that I expect things or money—or maybe that I expect different circumstances—to make me happy. If I just have a 14', 24-pound fiberglass kayak like Jim has, well then I'll be happy. If I just have an iPhone, then I'll be happy. If I just have $100K in my retirement account like Fred does, then I'll be happy. If I just had a new house like she has, then I'd be happy. If I just have a new whatever, then I'll be happy.

What did the 10th Commandment say? "You shall not covet your neighbor's house; you shall not covet your neighbor's wife, or his male servant, or his female servant, or his ox, or his donkey (I think that was the OT equivalent of a new car), or anything that is your neighbor's." Why would God say that? Because God knows that new stuff, more stuff, won't make you happy.

If you think stuff will make you happy, then I suggest you take a moment and remember back to the time that you got your last raise. Sure, it made you happy, at the time. Maybe really happy, for a while! But are you still celebrating that raise? Does it still make you happy? Or are you discontent about how long ago that raise was and now you're growing quite impatient for another raise? Or how about that new phone you got a year ago, remember, the one you wanted and shopped around for, the one that was the newest and the coolest—the one that isn't so new now or so cool now and you'd like to trade up to have one like Susie has?

Face it. Happiness leaks. Got that? Over time, you fill up your happiness bucket with all sorts of fun stuff, good stuff, stuff that makes you happy but, unfortunately, over time, your "happiness bucket" leaks. So if you expect money or a new car or a new job or a new husband to make you happy, prepare to be disappointed. Because happiness leaks.

Second, I think that my envy means that I'm looking for happiness in all the wrong places and missing the source of bigger, deeper, more satisfying, more enduring happiness. Jesus said "Seek first the kingdom of God, and his righteousness, and all these things—all this other stuff—will be given to you as well" (Matthew 6:31). Okay. So what's the Kingdom of God?

Well, it's not a place, like a city with walls around it, or a country with borders that you cross. The kingdom of God is wherever God rules, wherever—or I should say, in whomever—God "reigns like a king," wherever God is submitted to and acknowledged as supreme and sovereign, as in charge and in control. That's what Jesus meant when he said "The Kingdom of God is within you" (Luke 17:20, 21).

> *Face it.*
> *Happiness leaks.*

So, seek first the rule and reign of God in your life. Let me break that down for a moment, try to unpack that:

Seek—diligently look for, search for, pursue—and then submit yourself to—then put yourself under the rule and control of God in all you do, in your wants and desires, in your ambitions and your goals, in your priorities and your values. Seek first the Kingdom of God and his righteousness—obey him, that's what seeking his righteousness means. Righteousness = right living. Pursue the right-living that pleases God. Do that first, and then all these other things, all the stuff that so consumes you and occupies your desires, all the stuff that eats up your resources of time and treasure, if you seek after God and his righteousness first, then all that other stuff will fall into its proper place in your life.

How do you do that? How do you seek the kingdom of God first? How do you seek his right-living first? Well, here are three steps in the path of seeking the rule of God in your life and seeking the right-living of God in your life. Got your pen? The first step on the path of seeking the rule and right-living of God in your life is...

Admitting that you are not God and that you need a savior. You can't submit to God if you are still thinking that you are God. You can't submit to the rule of God if you are still thinking that you are good enough just the way you are (maybe with a few tweaks here and there) to have a relationship with him.

I don't want to be rude to you or mean or harsh, but, if you haven't noticed, you're not God. And you're not good enough in any way at any time to have a relationship with God. If it makes you feel any better, neither am I. No one is.

"All have sinned and all fall short of the glory or perfect standard of God" (Romans 3:23; see Isaiah 59:2; 64:6). So the first step on the path to seeking the rule and right-living of God in your life is admitting that you're not God and that you need a savior.

Second step: Submit to Jesus as the one and only Son of God who loves you; the one who left heaven and came to earth to die in your place, and satisfy all the wrath of God that you deserve for your sin, and then rose again from the grave. Astounding. Incomprehensibly unscientific. Historically true.

Stop trying to be good enough, to save yourself, and instead, trust Jesus. Jesus only. Not Jesus plus being a good person. Not Jesus plus being really, really intelligent. Not Jesus plus going to church. Not Jesus plus having parents who are Christians. No, trusting Jesus—and Jesus only—to save you.

If the first step on the path to seeking the rule and right-living of God in your life is admitting that you're not God and that you need a savior, and the second step on the path to seeking the rule and right-living of God in your life is trusting Jesus only to save you, then what's Step 3?

Step three is submitting each and every day—and every part of those days—to the rule and reign of God in your life. How do you do that? First, start each day with prayer. "Lord, I love you and I need your help today if I am going to please you!"

I like to begin with what people call the Lord's Prayer, I think of it as the Disciple's Prayer. "Our Father—that's acknowledging that 'God, you made me and I am your child;' our Father, who is in heaven—that's 'You're God, I'm not.' Hallowed, or Holy is your name—that's 'There is no god like you, there is no god besides you.' Your kingdom come, your will be done on earth as it is in heaven—that's 'God, please rule and reign in my life here in Attleboro today, be in control of my life at home and at work, in my conversations and projects, rule and reign in my day and my life for your glory, here, just like you rule and reign in heaven.'

> *"Our Father in heaven, hallowed be your name, your kingdom come, your will be done on earth as it is in heaven..."*
>
> Jesus
> Matthew 6:9, 10

To seek first the kingdom of God and his right-living, his righteousness, is to begin the day with submissive prayer. And then throughout the day continue to submit yourself to the rule and reign of God— at school or at work, at home or on the field, at the gym and in the supermarket. Everywhere, in all things, at all times. Seek first, the kingdom of God and his righteousness and all of these other things will fall into their proper place.

If I am talking to God throughout the day about my conversations, my appointments, my relationships, then I see that cute girl at the gym not as a sexual object but as a woman made in the image of God who is loved by God and needs to know personally the God who made and loves her. If I am talking to God throughout the day about my conversations and appointments, my decisions and my opportunities, then the iPad that Jeff shows me is just a thing. A thing that will leak happiness. And I have bigger priorities in the day than getting yet another thing that leaks.

This God-centered life, this Jesus-serving life that I'm talking about is what the Bible means when it says "Godliness with contentment is great gain" (1 Timothy 6:6). You're way ahead of the curve. You've mastered something in life that few others have mastered if you are living a God-centered, Jesus-serving life that is content.

Happiness leaks.

But godliness with contentment is great gain.

So, if I asked you about contentment—the corresponding virtue of envy—on a scale of 1-10, where 10 is blissfully content with your life and 1 is being eaten up by envy, where are you right now? Okay, so I'm not saying you should not finish your education. And I'm not saying you should not apply for that promotion. I'm not saying that you should stay in that abusive relationship. There is such a thing as holy, sanctified ambition. No, I'm talking here about envy *vs.* contentment. Where are you, 1 to 10?

How easy is it for you to be suckered in by ads, by fads, by peer pressure, by the newest and latest greatest toy? How easy is it for you to ignore the stuff and focus on seeking first the Kingdom of God and the right-living he wants for you? Happiness leaks—but Godliness with contentment is great gain. Take a moment before you turn to the next page and reflect on what God is saying to you through his word today.

Digging deeper...

1. Steve wrote "happiness leaks." Think for a moment about something that you really wanted and finally got. How is that happiness holding up or is it leaking? Tell that story here...

2. Matthew 6:33 tells us to "Seek first the Kingdom of God and his righteousness and all these other things will be given to you." Reflect for a moment on how you are seeking the Kingdom of God (the rule and reign of God in your life) and pursuing his righteousness (right-living). Write your thoughts here...

3. Read Exodus 20:17 and 1 Timothy 6:6. How are you doing with "Godliness with contentment brings great gain?" Would you say that you are content? Why? If not, what is getting in the way of contentment in your life?

4. Assignment: Memorize Proverbs 14:30 and Job 5:2. Write them out on cards. Read them over. Say them out loud. Repeat. Pray them in your prayers.

CHAPTER 4

Ohhh!

But I tell you that anyone who looks at a woman lustfully has already committed adultery with her in his heart.
- Matthew 5:27

So the first chapter was about pride and we said that the antithesis of pride is humility. And humility is not thinking less of yourself but thinking of yourself less. In chapter two we talked about greed and we saw that the corresponding virtue is charity or outrageous, prodigal, extravagant generosity. We said God doesn't give you money to bless you; God gives you money to bless others. In chapter three we confronted envy and we said that happiness leaks—but godliness with contentment is great gain.

In this chapter I want to talk with you about something that is deep and personal and not at all easy to talk about. The topic is lust.

Lust is anything but harmless, victimless and innocent. Jesus said that lust in your heart is just the same as actual, physical adultery. Listen to what he said; we find it in

Matthew, chapter 5, verse 27: "You have heard that it was said, 'Do not commit adultery.' (Of course Jesus is quoting from the Ten Commandments here; Commandment number seven, Do not commit adultery.) But I tell you that anyone who looks at a woman lustfully has already committed adultery with her in his heart." That's pretty steep! That's pretty harsh! What man, what woman, hasn't looked at someone at some time lustfully? Did you notice how Jesus said it all begins with a lustful look? According to this standard by Jesus we're all adulterers!

I've written before in *Obeying Jesus* about how I was exposed to pornography for the first time in college and wrestled unsuccessfully for years with the temptation, and then the guilt, the feeling of dirtiness inside, and the hopelessness of failure after failure to get victory over the temptation.

Not only did messing with porn waste tons of time and some money, it messed with my view of women (and of myself!), it desensitized me to sin, it wrecked my relationship with God, and it made me a sneak and a liar, always hiding stuff, always afraid someone would find out, never being able to talk truthfully about how I spent some of my time. And, you know, in the process, I discovered two sad facts about porn. First, that it promises to satisfy, but it never does. It just leaves you wanting more. Second, I learned that porn is addictive in that like a drug, over time, it needs more porn or worse porn to have the same effect. You actually become dulled, inoculated, calloused to what you, at one time, would have thought was horrible or disgusting, and you go to debased places that you never would have imagined possible.

And porn was a very effective tool of Satan to take me out of the game and wreck me spiritually; making me feel guilty, dirty, worthless, powerless, unworthy of God's grace, and unworthy of serving him. Finally, after years of unsuccessful and discouraging struggles, I was finally rescued by God's grace through an in-depth, 60-day, online, guided bible study called Setting Captives Free.[6]

So I talk about that, knowing that it makes some of you uncomfortable. I'm sorry I'm making you uncomfortable. And I have learned that some respect me less for my past and for talking openly about it. So be it. But it's clear in the bible that leaders of churches need to be humbly transparent and authentic (James 5:16; see Ephesians 5:21), not fake and hypocritical; leaders need to be humble and accountable, not in some exalted, untouchable position. If we expect others to be authentic about who they really are—if we expect brothers and sisters in Christ to be honest and transparent about the things they struggle with and the help they need—then the example for that honesty and integrity has to start with, has to be modeled by, the leaders of the church. If we are going to establish a church-wide culture where fake spirituality and false fronts are *not* welcome, where honesty and transparency are valued, where hidden sins are exposed to

---

[6] Check out www.SettingCaptivesFree.com. There are great, free, online studies that help you with eating issues, porn, alcohol and drugs, self-injury, and gambling. Each study ends with an online assessment and a real person follows up with you by email to hold you accountable and support you as you wrestle with breaking free of overwhelming temptations.

the light of the truth of God's word, a church where grace is amazing and abundant, where sisters and brothers humbly help each other get up and grow up, and mature in Christ, then it has to start with the leaders.

Porn by the numbers...

Listen, if I thought I was the only one who ever had this problem with lust then maybe I wouldn't tell you my story. If I thought I was the only one who struggled with guilt and shame, with what felt like helplessness and hopelessness, then maybe I'd just keep it to myself. But look at these statistics...

- Average age of first internet exposure to pornography is 11 years old
- 90% of 8-16 year olds have viewed porn online, mostly while doing homework
- 80% of 15-17 year olds have had multiple hard-core porn exposures
- 20% of men admit to accessing pornography at work and 13% of women
- 70% of men 18-24 y.o. visit porn sites in an average month
- But 1 of 3 visitors to all adult web sites are women
- 17% of all women struggle with pornography addiction
- Women favor chat rooms 2X more than men,
- 56% of divorce cases involve one party having an obsessive interest in online porn

- 47% of Christians say porn is a major problem in their home[7]

Some of you might be reading this thinking it is totally inappropriate and wonder why we have to talk about this at all. Listen, I'm genuinely happy for you if lust is not an issue for you. I mean that. Praise God! But if that last number above is correct, 47%, then just about half of the homes represented by readers of this book would say that porn is a major issue in their homes. So I wasn't alone.

I don't have to tell you that we live in a lust saturated culture where I don't know where to look in the checkout isle at the supermarket because the explicit porn story titles on the cover of *Cosmo* in the magazine rack; where TV commercials, never mind the programs and movies, are filled with women as sexual objects or the aggressive players, and men are played out as pathetic, helpless animals controlled by their hormones, or worse yet, as predators. We live in a culture where sexting is pretty common among students: 18% of teen boys and 11% of young teen girls ages 13-16 have sent or posted nude or seminude pictures of themselves. We live in a hyper-sexualized culture where "friends with privileges" and the hooking-up culture make college campuses from coast to coast pretty uncomfortable and even unsafe for any who want to live in any semblance of purity. We live in a culture where adultery has lost its stain and stigma and is softened by our word choices like "having an affair," openly

[7] Sources: www.xxxchurch.com & www.covenanteyes.com

discussed and accepted as the common entertaining story line in movies and TV series—and thus accepted as normal with little discomfort in real life.

I think the advent of free chat rooms and anonymous porn on the internet has seduced millions of otherwise decent people. And e-readers like Kindle, Nook and iPads let otherwise respectable people surreptitiously download and read "Mommy porn" trash like "50 Shades of Gray" that they'd never show the cover of or leave out on the coffee table. And I think the advent of porn, particularly on the internet, has stolen the innocence of our children, has coarsened our society in general, has stimulated the surge in child sex abuse,[8] and is a huge step backward for the honor and respect of women in particular.

Jesus knows all about it, really!

So, what should you do, live in a cave? How does a follower of Jesus—someone who wants to please him by the life they lead, someone who wants to have consistent integrity in what they say they believe and what they actually do—how do you live in a culture that is intent on tempting you to lust at every turn?

Surprisingly—or maybe not so surprisingly—Jesus knows lust is a universal and timeless problem. Okay, so

---

[8] "In 2004, the Cyber Tipline received 106,119 reports, marking more than a thirty-fold increase in child pornography in a six-year period. In that period, the victims involved in the child pornography became younger and younger, and the sexual activity in the images became more graphic and extreme. Recent empirical studies also support the proposition that individuals who consume child pornography are often also child molesters, which suggests that the rise in volume of child pornography available online translates into a very real danger for children." Drew Osterbaan, *Internet Pornography and Child Exploitation,* Nov 2006, 54:7, p 1.

first century followers of Jesus didn't have the internet or Kindle, sexting or Youtube to deal with. But some of the pornographic frescoes on the walls of homes and businesses in the ancient buried Roman city of Pompeii and just uncovered by archeologists in the last century are so outrageous and so offensive that minors are still only allowed entry to some villas today in the presence of a guardian or with written permission. We didn't invent pornography—or lust. It's been around for millennia. Jesus spoke simply and clearly about it.

Look again with me at Matthew, chapter 5, starting at verse 27: "You have heard that it was said, 'Do not commit adultery.' But I tell you that anyone who looks at a woman lustfully has already committed adultery with her in his heart. If your right eye causes you to sin, gouge it out and throw it away. It is better for you to lose one part of your body than for your whole body to be thrown into hell. And if your right hand causes you to sin,[9] cut it off and throw it away. It is better for you to lose one part of your body than for your whole body to go into hell."

It's time for radical amputation...

Did you catch the context there? That whole "If your right eye causes you to sin, gouge it out and throw it away" thing is in the context of "But I tell you that anyone who looks at a woman lustfully has already committed adultery with

---

[9] Is it possible that in this context of lust Jesus is referring here to masturbation fueled by lustful, adulterous thoughts—"If your right hand causes you to sin, cut it off and throw it away!"—masturbation which in turn dwells on, intensifies, reinforces and rewards the lust-filled thoughts?

her in his heart." The strategy that Jesus suggested for dealing with the temptation of lust was what can only be called "Radical Amputation." If your eye causes you to sin, gouge it out.

Now to be sure, Jesus was using hyperbole here, he was using dramatic overstatement to make his point stick. He didn't really intend that totally committed disciples would be walking around with only one eye or one hand. But he did intend us to get the point of how serious the sin of lust is: "It is better for you to lose one part of your body than for your whole body to go into hell."

> *Jesus didn't really intend that totally committed disciples would be walking around with only one eye or one hand. But he did intend us to get the point of how serious the sin of lust is.*

Too often we rationalize, excuse and explain away lust just like we rationalize our other habits: "It's not that bad. I can handle it." (Implying it might be sin for you but, I can handle it without sinning.) Or have you heard this one, "I'm just appreciating God's creation!" — I've heard that one. Pretty spiritual, huh?

No, Jesus calls it like it is, sin. And he said we need to do radical amputation if we are going to survive. You remember the story of Aaron Ralston, the young hiker who, back in 2003, was doing what he normally does, he was hiking Blue John Canyon in Utah when the unimaginable happened; a large boulder became dislodged and trapped his right forearm against the canyon wall. No one knew where he had been heading that day, and he knew that no one would be searching for him. After four days with his arm trapped and running out of water Aaron came to a clear conclusion: if he was going to survive he had to amputate his trapped forearm himself. He did it. And he survived. Radical amputation.

Jesus said, cut off, amputate, anything that is trapping you, anything that is leading you into irresistible temptation, anything that is deadly for you. This whole concept of radical amputation was really liberating for me. For me it meant not carrying any cash; using a credit card for every transaction, from a pack of gum to a new power tool, so I was fully accountable to Deb for all my spending. It meant moving the family computer to the living room where the screen can be easily seen by anyone. It meant putting web-browsing accountability software on my laptop that records every site I visit and reports any questionable sites to my accountability partners. It meant having accountability partners, other guys who I told what was happening and asked them to push on me with tough questions, to force me out of isolation and secrecy and make me be accountable.

Some folks chuckle because I spend so much time at the local Panera Bread shop in North Attleboro; or maybe they question if that location is a wise use of my time—after all, how do you study the bible and write sermons at

Panera? But the alternative for me is to sit alone at the Chapel in my Study for hours and even days with no one watching what is on my laptop screen, with no one seeing how I spend my time. Been there and it's not good for me. At Panera, facing the wall, I've got dozens of people behind me who see my computer screen all day, every day, and they don't know it but they help keep me pure. And yes, I study and read and write sermons—and this book—at Panera. Some of you know that because you see me there, you stop over and chat. Now you know why I'm there. It's all part of an ongoing, never-ending campaign of radical amputation for me; doing what I have to do to totally wipe out, eradicate the temptation that wants to kill me.

6 tools to help you win...

If Cut, radical amputation, is one strategy, I want to give you five more, six tools total, to help you win, to have victory over lust. So Cut is first. The second is Stop. Look at Romans 13:13*ff* with me. The Apostle Paul is writing to followers of Jesus living in Rome, surely a liberal, cosmopolitan city in his day. And he writes, verse 13, "Let us behave decently, as in the daytime (that is, when the light is shining to expose all our acts for everyone to see), Let us behave decently, as in the daytime not in orgies and drunkenness, not in sexual immorality and debauchery, not in dissension and jealousy. Rather (instead), clothe yourselves with the Lord Jesus Christ, and do not think about how to gratify the desires of the sinful nature."

"Do not think about how to gratify the desires of the sinful nature!" The ESV says "make no provision for the flesh, to gratify its desire." What's that? Stop plotting. Stop planning. Stop planning ahead how you're going to feed your lust and get away with it. Stop making it easy. Stop window shopping for sin.

Why did you add HBO or Showtime to your cable subscription? Do you really need access to R-rated movies? Is that good for helping you grow to maturity in Christ? Really? Technology makes planning and plotting to sin easier than ever. "I'll download that book to my Kindle and no one will ever know what I'm reading." "I'll erase my browsing history." Listen, I know Windows makes that pretty easy to do but I'm not really sure there's ever any good reason to erase your browsing history, other than to hide your tracks. No, stop plotting. Stop planning. Stop thinking about how to gratify the desires of the sinful nature.

> **There is hope!**
>
> *No temptation has seized you except what is common to man. And God is faithful; he will not let you be tempted beyond what you can bear. But when you are tempted, he will also provide a way out so that you can stand up under it.*
>
> *- 1 Corinthians 10:13*

First, Cut. Second, Stop. Third, Run! Look at 2 Timothy 2:22. The Apostle Paul is writing to his young mentee, Timothy, coaching him on how to live and work for the Kingdom. Look at his advice in 2 Timothy, chapter 2, verse 2: "Flee the evil desires of youth, and (instead) pursue righteousness, faith, love and peace, along with those who call on the Lord out of a pure heart." Flee! Run!

Like Joseph, remember that story in Genesis 39? His employer's wife came on to him, tried to seduce him, and what did he do? Stand there and discuss it? Did he say, "Well, I can stay for a little while but I'll have to leave soon."? Did he say, "I can handle this!"? No, he ran.

What's going on in your life right now that you should be running away from? Not walking. Running! A situation at work with a hurting and lonely woman who needs a friend to listen to her story? Run! A roommate at school who likes to party and mess around? Run! A boyfriend—or a girlfriend—who ignores your desire to keep things clean by wearing stuff that just messes with you? Run!

Strategy number one: Cut. Strategy number two: Stop. Strategy number three: Run. Strategy number four is Get. Look at 1 Corinthians 15:33" "Do not be misled: 'Bad company corrupts good character.'" Isn't that obvious? Then why is it so hard?

Hanging around with the same crowd that you used to party with? That's just asking for trouble. Get some new friends. Hanging around with the same guy that introduced you to porn. Get new friends. I've heard some Christ-followers say, "But he's my oldest friend?" Or have you heard this one, "But maybe she'll become a Christian if I stay in this relationship?" They call that one Evangelistic Dating. Nope. Get new friends. Your old friend is not going to understand the message and the demands of the gospel if you are messed up in sin. Pray for them. But get new friends.

Number one, Cut. Number two, Stop. Number three, Run. Number four, Get. Number five, Pray. Sure, pray. You can make that Number one, too. Jesus told his disciples on the night he was betrayed, "Pray that you won't fall into temptation. The spirit is willing, but the body is weak" (Matthew 26:41).

You might have the best intentions, the best desires. You really, really want to please God. You really, really want to have victory over lust, porn, whatever. Jesus knows all about that and he knows that the spirit is willing, but the body is weak and so he says you better pray.

Listen, it's pretty hard to click on that web site if you are praying for strength and courage and victory over lust at that moment. It's pretty hard to be lusting for that girl if you're praying for her, thanking God for her and praying for her salvation and spiritual growth. Jesus says, pray.

Number six, Think. Philippians, chapter 4, verse 8: "Finally, brothers, whatever is true, whatever is noble, whatever is right, whatever is pure, whatever is lovely, whatever is admirable—if anything is excellent or praiseworthy—think about such things." If lust is the sin, the corresponding virtue is purity. And you get to purity by changing what you think about. Whatever is true—she's not a sexual object to be had. She's a woman made in the image of God, loved by God, who needs to know God's love for her. Whatever is noble—is that good thought, a noble thought? Or is that disgusting? Whatever is right, pure—would you like it if everyone knew that was what you were watching or listening to or reading?

Change the music you listen to and sing along to because that is putting thoughts and values in your head. Change the TV shows you watch. Change the web sites you visit. The old saying, GIGO, "Garbage in; garbage out" still applies. Instead, fill you mind with positive, helpful, hopeful, good things, not trash. "Whatever is right, whatever is pure, whatever is lovely, whatever is admirable—if anything is excellent or praiseworthy—think about such things."

Cut, Stop, Run. Get, Pray, Think. Read that out loud with me: *Cut, Stop, Run. Get, Pray, Think.* Six strategies. Six tools. Pick one, any one. Pick two. Whatever. They're useful in dealing with the lust in your life. And actually, they're useful for dealing with any temptation, any habit, any besetting sin in your life, not just lust.

So let's talk for a moment. What are you wrestling today? Okay, the statistics say that Christians have as much a problem with porn as anyone else. So maybe your issue is porn. Or gambling. Or pride. Or cutting. Or food. Or envy that we talked about in the last chapter. Or maybe it's alcohol or abusing prescription drugs. Or maybe for you it's anger and control, manipulation and intimidation. Maybe it's something else.

Well, the good news is that Jesus died for that sin. He died to take on himself the full wrath of the holy God, wrath that you deserved for that sin, and to cleanse you from all uncleanness, to give you new life, new hope and a new future. And if you are a believer in Jesus, he sent you the Holy Spirit to convict you of that sin (John 16:8)—to make you miserable, to give you no peace and no rest until you confess it as sin and cry out for forgiveness and help. Lust, like all sin, is first and foremost a spiritual issue.

Listen, Jesus is there with you as you read this. He loves you with an everlasting love, more deeply than anyone has ever loved you. As Philip Yancy wrote, "Grace means there's nothing I can do to make God love me more; and nothing I can do to make God love me less."[10] He will hear your prayer right now; your prayer of confession, your prayer for forgiveness, your prayer for cleansing. And he is waiting for you to turn to him for help in getting free from whatever it is that has you enslaved right now. Take a few quiet moments and talk with Jesus now.

---

[10] Philip Yancy. *What's so amazing about grace?* (Grand Rapids: Zondervan, 2007), 71.

Digging deeper...

1. Jesus said "Whoever has looked at a woman lustfully has already committed adultery with her in his heart" (Mt. 5:27). Wow! That's pretty convicting. Do you need to confess the sin of lust and repent? Take time now to have that conversation with God. Name your sin. Ask for forgiveness. Write out 1 John 1:9 here and believe it.

2. Is pornography an issue in your life? Of someone close to you? Steve wrote "There is hope!" (p. 48). Based on the truth and the promise found in 1 Corinthians 10:13, what is that hope for you?

3. Steve listed six bible-based tools to help you get free of porn. Write out exactly how you plan to use each tool to fight the temptation of porn — or whatever the temptation is for you.

- *Cut*, "Radical Amputation" of anything that makes it easy to fall to temptation (Matthew 5:29, 30)

- **Stop** planning ahead to feed your lust and get away with it (Romans 13:12-14)

- **Run** fast from any situation, or relationship, or activity that feeds temptation (2 Timothy 2:22)

- **Get** new friends who will support your new values (1 Corinthians 15:33)

- **Pray** that you resist temptation (Matthew 26:41)

- **Think** about positive, good things, not junk (Philippians 4:8)

CHAPTER 5

Whatever

Go to the ant, you sluggard;
consider its ways and be wise.
It has no commander, no overseer or ruler,
yet it stores its provisions in summer
and gathers its food at harvest.

- Proverbs 6:6

Here's a quick review. The first chapter was about pride and we said that the antithesis of pride is humility. And humility is not thinking less of yourself but thinking of yourself less. In chapter two we talked about greed and we saw that the corresponding virtue is charity or outrageous, prodigal, extravagant generosity. We said God doesn't give you money to bless you; God gives you money to bless others. The third chapter was about envy and we said that happiness leaks—but godliness with contentment is great gain.

Then in the last chapter we talked about lust and the corresponding virtue, purity. And I gave you six biblical tools, six strategies for dealing with the lust—or any other sinful habit—in your life. Six strategies: C-S-R, G-P-T. *Cut, Stop, Run. Get, Pray, Think.*

In this chapter we're exploring number five, a strange vice on our list of The Seven Deadly sins. We're talking about sloth. No, not the fuzzy, cute, little, South American, three-toed, tree sloth! Sloth as in sluggard; you know, a lazy, indolent, lethargic, languid (I always wanted to be able to use that word, languid, in a sentence: it sounds like what it means, *lan-guid*), we're talking about an apathetic slacker. Our English word sloth comes from a Greek word that means, "without care." We could say that sloth is the sin of care-less-ness, as in "I couldn't possibly care less..."

Now maybe you know a thing or two about sloth, a bit about care-less-ness, already. I want to talk with you about four special kinds of sloth. The bible gives us a few examples that might ring a bell. Turn with me to the middle of your bible, to the book of Proverbs, chapter 6. Proverbs is a collection of short, wise sayings; look with me down at verse 6: "Go to the ant, you sluggard; consider its ways and be wise. It has no commander, no overseer or ruler, yet it stores its provisions in summer and gathers its food at harvest."

You remember Disney's movie, *A Bug's Life*. Ants working hard to store up food. So the proverb says "Go to the ant, you sluggard (isn't that a great word, *sluggard!*) Go to the ant, you sluggard; consider its ways and be wise. It has no commander, no overseer or ruler, yet it stores its provisions in summer and gathers its food at harvest"

(Proverbs 6:6-8). When most of us think about sloth, we think of a lazy person who refuses to work, vegging out on the couch, life drifting away while they're playing games on Facebook.

The Bible has a lot to say about this kind of sloth. "How long will you lie there, you sluggard? When will you get up from your sleep? A little sleep, a little slumber, a little folding of the hands to rest—and poverty will come on you like a bandit and scarcity like an armed man" (Proverbs 6: 9-11). "The sluggard buries his hand in the dish and will not even bring it back to his mouth" (Proverbs 19:24). "The sluggard says, 'There is a lion outside! I shall be killed in the streets!'" (Proverbs 22:13). Always making excuses why they can't get up and get to work; excuses that are so transparent and so obvious to everyone; they're not really fooling anyone except maybe themselves.

The Apostle Paul responds "If anyone is not willing to work, let him not eat." It's clear from the Bible that work, even hard work, even two jobs if that's what it takes to put food on the table, is expected of anyone who calls themselves a follower of Jesus. Turn with me to 2 Thessalonians chapter 3 so we can look at the context around that statement, "If anyone is not willing to work, let him not eat."

2 Thessalonians, chapter 3, we're reading from verse 6: "In the name of the Lord Jesus Christ, we command you, brothers, to keep away from every brother who is idle and does not live according to the teaching you received from us. For you yourselves know how you ought to follow our

example. We were not idle when we were with you, nor did we eat anyone's food without paying for it. On the contrary, we worked night and day, laboring and toiling so that we would not be a burden to any of you. (Paul was a tent-maker, supporting himself with a day job) We did this, (supporting ourselves with our own work, Paul writes) not because we do not have the right to such help, but in order to make ourselves a model for you to follow. For even when we were with you, we gave you this rule: 'If a man will not work, he shall not eat.' We hear that some among you are idle. They are not busy; they are busybodies. Such people we command and urge in the Lord Jesus Christ to settle down and earn the bread they eat. And as for you, brothers, never tire of doing what is right. If anyone does not obey our instruction in this letter, take special note of him. Do not associate with him, in order that he may feel ashamed. Yet do not regard him as an enemy, but warn him as a brother." Pretty stiff stuff!

There should never be a follower of Jesus who isn't doing all that he or she can do—no excuses—to provide for themselves and their family. Again Paul writes "Make it your ambition to lead a quiet life, to mind your own business, and to work with your hands, just as we told you, so that your daily life may win the respect of outsiders and so that you will not be dependent on anybody" (1 Thessalonians 4:11-12).

Listen to 1 Timothy, chapter 5: "If any man does not provide for his relatives, and especially for his immediate family, he has denied the faith (Wow!) and is worse than an unbeliever." "If any woman who is a believer has widows in her family, she should help them and not let the church be burdened with them, so that the church can help those widows who are really in need." The principle here brothers and sisters: we all have a responsibility to work hard, to care for ourselves and for our family so that we and they are not a burden to anyone.

And that goes against the grain of a culture that is increasingly willing to be shamelessly dependent on someone else—usually some government program or the generosity of strangers—with a long list of reasons why they can't work. The one that really gets my goat is "I'll lose my benefits if I take a job!" With 56% of the federal budget going to entitlement programs, and 40 cents of every one of those entitlement dollars borrowed from our grandchildren who will have to pay it back with interest, it's time to get back to the principle of personal responsibility that says: "Get to work or don't eat!"

I know there are some unfortunate souls who can't work due to illness, and some are retired, and I know that jobs are tight right now; I understand that. But with nearly half—49.5%—of the population not paying any income taxes at all on one hand, combined with the inequity of huge US corporations taking their profits offshore and getting corporate welfare in the form of bailouts, subsidies and tax breaks on the other, we have a growing culture, a habit, an unsustainable addiction to an entitlement/dependence mentality that will come to ruin sooner rather than later. Think Greece. Think Spain. Don't think it can't happen in America. The clock is ticking.

Beyond feeding yourself and your family, the goal for followers of Jesus is also to work so that you can be in a position to help others, each "...must work, doing something useful with his own hands, that he may have something to share with those in need" (Ephesians 4:28; see Galatians 6:10).

The Christian work ethic...

So it is simple and clear that the bible says, get to work; followers of Jesus should be givers, not takers. But there is a second kind of sloth that the bible talks about. Turn again to Proverbs in the middle of your bible; the wisdom sayings of the OT. Look at Proverbs, chapter 10, look down at verse 26: "As vinegar to the teeth and smoke to the eyes, so is a sluggard to those who send him." Vinegar irritates the teeth just like smoke irritates your eyes; just like a sluggard on the job irritates anyone who gives them an assignment but knows that they'll drag their feet, whine and complain while they pretend to work, make all sorts of excuses why the task is too hard or that the assignment is unfair, and then deliver poor work, late, or maybe not at all.

Do you know anyone like that? Maybe someone you work with? Maybe one of your own kids? Maybe actually you suspect that your coworkers think that describes you? Again, Scripture speaks clearly to a solid work ethic. Turn with me to Colossians at the back of your bible, Paul's short letter to the church in Colossi, Colossians, chapter 3, look down at verse 22: "Slaves, obey your earthly masters in everything; and do it, not only when their eye is on you and to win their favor, but with sincerity of heart and reverence for the Lord. Whatever you do, work at it with all your heart, as working for the Lord, not for men..."

Paul is writing to the *dulos*, the slaves, bondservants, the working class of his day, and he says: Obey your employer in everything; and do it, not only when their eye is on you and to win their favor (Do it not only when you are being watched but even when you are not being watched), do it with sincerity of heart (with good intentions, with honesty and integrity) and with reverence for the Lord. And whatever you do, work at it with all your heart—work hard, do good work—as working for the Lord, not for men."

> **The Christian Work Ethic:**
>
> *Whatever you do, work at it with all your heart, as working for the Lord, not for men.*
>
> *- Colossians 3:22*

That's the Christian work ethic. "Whatever you do, work at it with all your heart as working for the Lord, not for men." Ultimately, you and I will answer to God—not to our supervisor, not to our union steward, not to the job foreman, but to God, for our work. Christians should be model employees. Showing up on time and ready to work. Staying until the job is done right, not skipping out early. Bringing a good attitude to the workplace; not griping or making excuses. Willing to do what is asked and needed without complaint. Team players who work extra hard to get along well with the rest of the team; showing grace to those who need grace. Watching our language, our conversations, our attitudes since they reflect not only on us but on other Christians, on the name of Christ, even on your church family.

The follower of Jesus is humble in the workplace, not stealing someone's work or taking credit for someone else's work. Giving credit to the team when there's success; taking responsibility for failure. Jim Collins calls that "The window and the mirror" approach in his business classic, *Good to Great*:[11] when things go well, "look out the window" at the team who made it possible. When things go bad, "look in the mirror" and take personal responsibility without blaming others. Simple, basic principles of being a good employee apply to followers of Jesus like leaving the workplace neater and better than the way you found it. Offering to help others when you have a moment rather than sitting there watching them struggle. Instead of over-promising and under-delivering; under-promising and over-delivering.

Okay, that's all simple stuff that your dad or the Boy Scouts might have taught you. But stuff that is so obviously missing in our "Protect my rights," "Not my job, man" culture. Christ-followers should be different, should be

---

[11] Collins, Jim *Good to Great: Why some companies make the leap..and others don't* (New York: Harper Business, 2001).

model employees, should be excellent bosses: "Whatever you do, work at it with all your heart, as working for the Lord, not for men..."

Not so obvious but subtle and dangerous...

So the first kind of sloth is avoiding work. The second kind of sloth is working badly. There is also a third kind of sloth that the Bible talks about. And this one is not quite so obvious, is much more subtle, and even more dangerous. It's the sloth of a parent who puts off, ignores, or delegates the training of their child. The guy who puts the kids to bed early so he can get back to his video games or his favorite sports team. It's the parents who watch a TV show or a movie with the kids but skip the opportunity to talk about the issues or morals, the lessons that surface in that show or movie. It's the parents who expect the Christian School, the Sunday School, or the Youth Group to teach their children about Jesus and the foundational spiritual disciplines of bible reading and prayer.

Turn to Deuteronomy, the fifth book at the front of your bible, Deuteronomy, chapter 6. Find verse 4: "Hear, O Israel: The LORD our God, the LORD is one. Love the Lord your God with all your heart and with all your soul and with all your strength. These commandments that I give you today are to be upon your hearts. Impress them on your children. Talk about them when you sit at home and when you walk along the road, when you lie down and when you get up. Tie them as symbols on your hands and bind them on your foreheads. Write them on the doorframes of your houses and on your gates."

This is a classic text. Underline this one, from verse 4 through verse 9, in your Bible. Notice what is missing here? Sure. No Sunday School. No Youth Group. Whose job is it to teach the kids? Dad and mom. What's the assignment? Impress the basic truths about God, who he is, loving him with all your heart, soul and strength; impress this on your children. How do you do that? You talk about it. When you get up; early in the morning as they're getting up and getting ready for their day, pray with them about the day ahead, teach them to thank God for the health and strength and freedom they have. Teach them to look for God at work in their life and their world.

Talk about this when you're at home, living life, doing life together in the house; talk about this on the way, in the car. Deb and I got some good kids tapes—old school, I know—with songs that we sang together over and over and over in the car, teaching bible verses, teaching truths about Jesus, instead of the stuff that's on the radio. I don't think our kids ever heard the radio in our car, unless maybe it was Focus on the Family. As the kids got older, the tapes and then the CDs changed. But all good, God-centered stuff chosen for and aimed at the captive audience in the back seat.

"When you lie down..." that's getting ready for bed. So Deb and I had a ritual that began in the infancy of our kids. Hold them and sing "Jesus Loves Me" and tell them a bible story and pray with them every night. As they got older, we switched to a children's story bible, we wore it out. As they got older, the version changed again. I like *The Action Bible* (published by D.C. Cook) available at Christian bookstores, on Amazon, and even Walmart. Chapter by chapter through the bible, every night. In their teen years, Middle School and High School, every night. The stories changed again as they got older, switched to reading the Bible through, still praying with them, and coaching them to pray, every night until graduation. Wear it on your clothes, hang it on your walls and doors.

Looking back, I regret that I didn't teach my children how to actually study the bible for themselves, not just read it. And I regret that I didn't teach them to keep a journal of their thoughts with the answers to their prayers and the things that they were feeling and learning about God. I regret that I missed that opportunity. But you, if you're a parent reading this today, you don't have to miss that opportunity.

One of the single most important things that Deb and I did to train up our children ourselves was our own example of being at Chapel with them every single Sunday. On time. With their bible in hand. No excuses. It was the single non-negotiable priority on the schedule every week, not an option. It's just what our family did. It is what family life centered around. It was a commitment, not a choice. What was that? That was training. Training in God-first priorities. Training in keeping a commitment. Training in responsibility.

Setting priorities...

Listen, don't expect your kids to place a top priority on worshipping God if you don't. If they see you choosing which Sunday to go to Chapel and which Sunday to sleep in, guess what lesson you just taught them? Sure, personal comfort and convenience is more important than worshipping God! If they see you coming to Chapel late, no bible, no offering ready for the bag when it passes, guess what lesson you just taught them? Sure, this isn't really all that important, just make a showing sometime.

If your kids see you making excuses why they should go to Chapel but you should stay home, guess what lesson you just taught them? Sure, you're lazy and undisciplined, you stayed up too late last night, and they should do what you say, not what you do. If you tell them that soccer or Little League or football is more important on Sunday morning than Sunday School; if you tell them that sports and homework are more important than Youth Group, guess what lesson you just taught them? Sure. God is second place to sports. Sports trumps God. Cool! Nice life lesson for the kids! (hint: sarcasm) And then you might wonder why they wander from the faith in their teen years, never go to church while they are away at college, and never return to church after college. *Surrrr-pri-se*!

Ignore this at your own risk...

While we're at it, there's one final special kind of sloth we need to talk out. First, the sloth of avoiding work. Second, the sloth of working badly. Third, the sloth of neglecting spiritual responsibilities in raising your kids. And finally, the sloth of ignoring your own spiritual health and growth.

C. S. Lewis recognized the power of this sin and wrote about it with his usual wit and piercing insight in his classic fiction, *The Screwtape Letters*. In *The Screwtape Letters*, the senior demon is named Screwtape, and he's instructing his nephew, Wormwood, who is a demon-in-training, an apprentice demon, how to draw his "patient," a young man named Chris, away from God. And in his twelfth letter to Wormwood, "uncle Screwtape" notes that "encouraging small sins can be more effective than encouraging great ones if they draw the Christian away from meaningful engagement with 'the enemy' (their name for God) without his realizing it." Listen to uncle Screwtape's instructions to his apprentice, Wormwood, from chapter 12...

> "As things progress, you will no longer need a good book, which he really likes, to keep him from his prayers . . . a column of advertisements in yesterday's paper will do. After a while you can make him do nothing at all for long periods. You can keep him up late at night, not roistering, but staring at a dead fire in a cold room. All the healthy and outgoing activities which we want him to avoid can be inhibited and nothing given in return."

7 Tools to help build your spiritual growth...
So what would it look like if you took responsibility for your own spiritual feeding, your own spiritual growth,

seriously? Let me suggest seven tools you can use to build your own spiritual growth and relationship with God.

First, some daily tools. Commit to reading the bible every day. In paper. On your phone or iPad or Kindle. An audio book that is someone reading to you. Whatever. Read through the Bible in a year. Or re-read a single book multiple times like John or James, Proverbs or Psalms and then pick another. Whatever. Just get reading. Begin to soak in the Word of God. Fill your mind with the Word of God. Let the words of God-centered truth begin to seep into your unconscious and inform your priorities, your values and your desires—and begin to push out the lies of the culture around us.

Second, develop a habit of pausing, multiple times throughout the day to pray. Not just when you get up, not just when you go to bed, not just at meals. Be like Daniel who set aside time three times a day just for prayer. I like Tevye, the Jewish father in "Fiddler on the Roof," walking along, pulling his milk wagon, talking, holding a day-long, ongoing conversation with God. Try applying the A-C-T-S model of prayer: Adoration, Confession, Thanksgiving, and Supplication.

Number three: be in a good Christ-exalting, bible-teaching, gospel-preaching church every Sunday. Make it a priority, a commitment, an investment. No excuses.

Fourth, commit to a weekly small group bible study for making new friends, a group of Jesus-followers praying with you and for you, studying the bible together and getting your questions answered. When you do life together with a group of fellow pilgrims on the path of following Jesus it is always more fun, more encouraging, more helpful.

Fifth, learn how to study the bible for yourself so that you are not dependent on someone else like me to teach you. Take an online course in Bible Study Methods to learn the skills.[12] Or ask one of the elders in your church or the person who leads your small group to teach you how to do it. Or you can get a good book like Rick Warren's excellent, simple, readable guide called *Bible Study Methods*. It equips you with not just one, but twelve methods for digging down, exploring all the stuff of God's Word. At least one of the 12 is exactly what you're looking for—an approach that's right for you, right where you're at. It's a simple step-by-step instruction guide you through the how-to's of studying the bible for yourself.

Tool number six: read a good book. Commit yourself to read one good Christian book, not Christian fiction, this month. Take your time. Read it slow. Read it twice. Underline and scribble some notes about your questions or your insights out in the margins. Not sure what to read? Ask a reader, "What's a good book I should read?" How about Henry Blackaby's "Experiencing God." How about Philip Yancy's "What's so Amazing About Grace?" What about "Crazy Love" by Francis Chan or "When God's People Pray" by Jim Cymbala or "Radical" by David Platt? Maybe a

---

[12] Gordon-Conwell Theological Seminary offers a free online course, *Studying the Bible for All Its Worth*, with Dr. Douglas Stuart. Check it out at http/my.gordonconwell.edu/page.aspx?pid=416. Other online options include Southern California Seminary's course in *Inductive Bible Study* (ED-3110). Check it out at http://socalsem.edu/online.

good biography like the life of Amy Carmichael or Jim Elliott.

Finally, tool number seven, set aside personal time to invest in your own spiritual growth every year: pick a conference to go to and hear great Bible teachers or to work on your marriage; or plan a personal spiritual retreat where you can look forward to some solitude and silence at least one day a year to review your spiritual journal, spend time resting, going for a walk, talking or writing or painting or singing to God, or meditating on a Psalm. Or plan and budget ahead to be part of a short-term mission team to support a local mission work and to stretch yourself in serving God and serving people Invest in your own spiritual growth. Make it happen by scheduling it on your calendar.

Okay, that was a ton of stuff. Now for the take-home question. On the Sloth/Sluggard Scale of 1-5, where are you? Before you turn the page, pause for a few minutes and consider what God wants to say to you today through his word about sloth.

Digging deeper...

1. Write out the Christian Work Ethic (p. 61) from Colossians 5:22 here:

2. Steve wrote about four kinds of sloth. The first was avoiding work. The second was working badly. The third was... Find it on page 63 and write it out here. Is that an issue for you? How can you help in this area?

3. Steve also listed a fourth kind of sloth (p. 66)—neglecting your own spiritual growth. Then he listed seven tools to nurture your growth. Which of those seven tools do you want to begin using? Explain that here...

4. Assignment: memorize 1 Thessalonians 4:11, 12

CHAPTER 6

Urrrgh!

In your anger do not sin.
Do not let the sun go down while you are still angry,
and do not give the devil a foothold.

- Ephesians 4:26

A couple of quick observations from Ephesians 4:26. First, Paul writes, "In your anger do not sin." Notice he doesn't say, "Never get angry." We all get angry at times. But there are different kinds of anger. There is justified anger, like anger at injustice. Remember how Jesus got angry and threw out the currency exchange dealers who were making a huge profit off the pilgrims who came to the Temple in Jerusalem during the feasts there (Matthew 21:12). There is a time and a place for righteous anger, particularly at injustice.

But there is also unjustified anger. The Apostle Paul calls that sin. I know that I am unjustified when I respond with anger to getting caught doing something I shouldn't be doing—like speeding. And how often do we respond to inconvenience, or disagreement, or misunderstanding with anger?

Some say "That's just the way I am, I can't help it." Others use the excuse "I have a short fuse, just like my dad." Some grew up in a home where anger was common, was expected, was the natural response that you learned to try to avoid but you lived with every day. You don't have to live like that.

Four new skills to control your anger...

There are four simple skills that you can learn to break free of your pattern, your habit, of anger. First of course is to admit that you have a problem with anger. Name it. Own it. Don't deny it. Don't excuse it. Don't rationalize it. Don't blame it on someone else: She made me angry! Really? Another person actually determines how you think and act? Another person is in your head? Really? No, you choose your own emotions.

Have you ever heard someone talking loudly or even yelling in the middle of a heated argument, their phone rings and they sweetly answer it, "*Hel-lo!*"? What does that tell you? Sure, they choose their emotions and responses. So first, name it, own it, admit you have a problem called anger. Confess it as sin against God and ask for his forgiveness.

Second, learn to identify the triggers: what pushes your buttons? What is it that brings on your response of anger? Is it always around money stuff? Is it around parenting issues? Is it about sex? Is it about household chores? Is it about your in-laws? Is it a certain guy at work who gets under your skin? What sets you off? Make a list, a chart with dates and events, figure it out. So learn to identify the triggers for you. Self-awareness is key.

Third, practice some new responses. We all tend to react with the same well-learned, well-rehearsed response when we find ourselves in similar circumstances. It becomes the default response. You don't even think about it, it just happens. But your response doesn't have to be anger. For example, you can train yourself to close your eyes and take 10 deep breathes. Slow, deep, cleansing breaths help change the physiology of anger, reducing your heart rate, lowering your blood pressure. Just pausing to "take a breath," to take breaths slowly and deeply for a few moments, can help clear your head for a more rational conversation.

And you can also learn to change your mental picture; choose to think about something that is good. Take the apostle Paul's advice, "What is true, whatever is noble, whatever is right, whatever is pure, whatever is lovely, whatever is admirable—if anything is excellent or praiseworthy—think about these things" (Philippians 5:8). I like to call up the mental picture of the small secluded beach on the north shore of Newfound Lake in New Hampshire, the site of many relaxing and fun family vacations. That mental image is very "pure, lovely and admirable" and calming for me.

So, practice new responses. I say "practice" because it will take a deliberate, intentional choice to practice new responses instead of just defaulting to the usual habit of uncontrolled, angry outbursts.

Fourth, learn to choose to give yourself a time out. You do that with kids when they are getting out of hand; you can do it with yourself. Say, "Can we continue this conversation later? I really need to calm down. How about we talk again after supper?" Be sure to make a date to resume the conversation and then take a walk or go to the gym, spend some time praying, reading a favorite Psalm, listening to some good Praise & Worship music; calm down, "take every thought captive, bring it into submission to Christ" (2 Corinthians 10:5).

> *Unresolved anger becomes resentment, and resentment becomes bitterness, and bitterness ultimately becomes hatred. And hatred kills, starting with you first.*

The consequences of unresolved anger...

Back to our verse in Ephesians 4: Paul says, go ahead, be angry (for a good reason), but then notice that he writes, "Don't let the sun go down on your wrath." What's that? Deal with it. Talk it out. Resolve it. Bring closure to it. Look for the Win/Win.

Because if you don't deal with it, your hostility, your suspicion, your anger will raise your heart rate and your blood pressure, it will keep you awake, you'll be grinding your teeth when you do get to sleep, you'll experience muscle tension and numbness, headaches, sweating, abdominal pain: it will wreck your health as well as your relationships at home and at work.

In the longer term, anger increases your risk of stroke, plus serious heart and abdominal issues. "For many women, constant suppressed anger seems to be a stronger risk factor for early mortality than smoking," said Dr. Mara Julius, an epidemiologist at the University of Michigan. "Our studies indicate that hostile, suspicious anger is right up there with any other health hazard we know about," said Dr. Redford Williams, a researcher in behavioral medicine at the Duke University Medical Center. Unresolved anger becomes resentment, and resentment becomes bitterness and bitterness ultimately becomes hatred. And hatred kills, starting with you first.

Another kind of anger...
But there is also another kind of anger that is not so obvious, at least in most churches, because it is usually well hidden, and only comes out to play behind closed doors at home. That's the anger that is deliberately chosen, deliberately used to control, to manipulate, to intimidate, to get your way in relationships. What is that? What's that all about? Simply? It's just selfishness. Plain and simple. Acting like a spoiled 2-year old. Throwing a tantrum to get your way. Being a bully to get people to do what you want. And nobody likes bullies. Nobody.

You know how it goes, someone doesn't agree with you so you say the same thing again, just louder this time. And when they still don't respond the way you want, you say the same thing even louder and with some choice cuss words. And when they still don't respond the way you want, you say it again, even louder now with more cussing and banging things. And when they still don't respond, you add a slap or a punch or a beating to the shouting and the cussing and the banging. An escalation. And somewhere in there you've crossed over from anger to abuse.

I want to talk with you about abuse, about domestic violence, for a few minutes. The cycle usually goes something like this. Typically, in Phase 1 tensions are building. There's a breakdown of communication. The victim becomes fearful and feels the need to placate the abuser. This is the "tip-toeing around on eggshells" phase, an attempt to keep everyone happy.

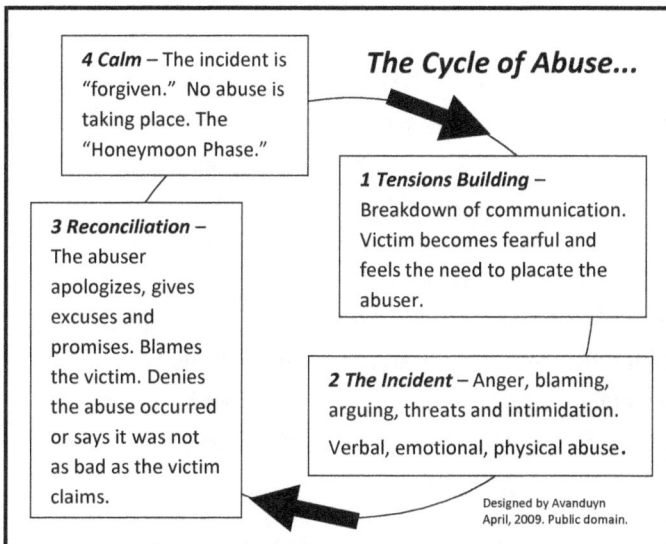

The Cycle of Abuse...

4 Calm – The incident is "forgiven." No abuse is taking place. The "Honeymoon Phase."

1 Tensions Building – Breakdown of communication. Victim becomes fearful and feels the need to placate the abuser.

3 Reconciliation – The abuser apologizes, gives excuses and promises. Blames the victim. Denies the abuse occurred or says it was not as bad as the victim claims.

2 The Incident – Anger, blaming, arguing, threats and intimidation. Verbal, emotional, physical abuse.

Designed by Avanduyn
April, 2009. Public domain.

In Phase 2 the Incident happens. The explosion. There's verbal, emotional, sexual, financial, and/or physical abuse. There's anger, blaming, arguing. Threats. Intimidation. Control. And sometimes violence.

In Phase 3, Reconciliation seems to happen. The abuser apologizes, sometimes very sincerely. And, the abuser usually gives excuses, frequently blaming the victim: "If you hadn't ..., then I wouldn't have to ..." Frequently the abuser denies the abuse ever occurred or tries to change the story by saying it wasn't really as bad as the victim claims.

And then there's Phase 4, the Calm Phase. The incident is "forgiven." No abuse is taking place at the moment. We're in the "Honeymoon phase," for a while until... Does that cycle, that pattern, sound at all familiar?

In the spring of 2012, I had the opportunity to interview Ruth Zakarin one Sunday morning at GNBC as part of a sermon that focused on domestic violence in this Deadly! series. Ruth was at the time the Vice President of Operations for *New Hope*, an Attleboro-based non-profit human service agency with over 30 years of experience in assisting people in crisis in Southern New England. Their mission is to work for ending domestic and sexual violence in dozens of surrounding communities. Ruth leads the "Alternatives to Shelter Task Force" that I served on at the time, developing emergency shelter options in the Greater Attleboro area communities for victims of domestic violence. So I interrupted the sermon and invited Ruth to sit together with me on the platform at the Chapel that

Sunday morning and I asked her a few questions that might be helpful to revisit here...

Steve – So, welcome Ruth! Thank you for being here! Can you talk with us about abuse for a moment? When we say abuse, or domestic violence, what exactly are we talking about; what's included in that picture?

Ruth – The definition we use for domestic violence is "A pattern of behaviors meant to control a person's partner through fear or hurt." And that can be a variety of things. Usually, when someone hears of domestic violence they first think of physical abuse which is certainly one component—but it is not the whole story when it comes to domestic violence.

There's also emotional or verbal abuse; putting people down, making them feel badly about themselves. There's of course sexual violence, often used in the context of an intimate relationship, to have power over a partner. But there's also financial abuse which is something most people are not that familiar with. If somebody is controlling the finances, or giving an allowance, or not giving someone access to the money that they or their children need to survive, that's a form of abuse as well.

There are also more specific kinds of abuse. For example, if someone is disabled, using their disability against them or using their immigration status against them—people can use a variety of tactics, in addition to physical violence, to make victims feel very fearful and feel that their options in life have been severely diminished and that is what I define as domestic violence.

Steve - Ruth, there might be a person here this morning who is asking the question in their mind, "How can I tell if my partner is abusive?" Maybe it's about them, or maybe their concern is about a family member or a friend. What are the warning signs that we should all be aware of?

Ruth – It is very likely, given the prevalence of domestic and sexual violence, that someone sitting here in this room has been affected, or knows someone who has been affected, by domestic or sexual violence, because it is unfortunately so widespread.

It really is about examining how you feel in a relationship and whether you feel that you have been disempowered; that your choices are being taken away from you, that you don't have a voice in your relationship. Whether it's because you fear physical retaliation, whether you feel you won't be given the money that you need to survive, whether you are afraid of being put down by your partner, minimized, having your work sabotaged, having partner do something to your children—all of those factors. If you are living in fear of what your partner will do to you if you don't behave correctly or meet their expectations, if you feel your choices are being taken away from you, that's a sign that you are in an unhealthy relationship.

Steve - So, I had a conversation last Sunday with Ray, a man who worships at Good News with his wife and their two sons. Ray asked me what the topic was going to be this morning in the Deadly! series. I told him it was Anger. He chuckled and said he was hoping it was going to be Gluttony today because he was going to be away this morning with his boys in New Hampshire at Berea's annual Father-Son Weekend.

But I asked Ray to pray with me this week about the talk today because I was going to talk about domestic violence, which I don't think has ever been a sermon topic at the Chapel before. Ray got very serious at that point. He's an MD, and a PhD, and he teaches surgery on the obstetrics faculty of Harvard Medical School. Ray quickly told me something I had never heard before: That pregnant women are at a very high risk of Domestic Violence and that the highest risk of DV for a woman is just after she has given birth. I was shocked by that but Ray sent me the statistics and some studies this week. Wow! Can you talk to us about that for a moment?

Ruth – It is hard to wrap your head around this but sadly it is in fact true. Sometimes we see situations where there may have already been a certain level of abuse happening in the relationship and a pregnancy escalates it; or there may not have been abuse before but all of a sudden during a pregnancy we start to see abuse things start to happen.

One of the reasons why that occurs is because pregnancy is a time when the abusive partner might not feel as much control over the victim because lots of things are happening, both to the person's body, and, they are out in the community more to get healthcare. And once the baby comes, suddenly everything is about the baby

81

because babies are all consuming, as everybody knows. At that time things can get very stressful in a relationship, partly because bringing a new baby into a home is stressful in itself, but also because the victim's energy is going towards the baby, not the abuser. And that is a loss of control for the abuser. And we know that violent relationships are all about power and control and anything that threatens that control tends to escalate the abuse.

Steve – It is very possible that someone is sitting here this morning and maybe for the first time they are putting "two plus two" together and they're saying, "Wow, I'm in an abusive relationship!" Do you have anything to say to them?

Ruth – Yes, I have a lot to say, actually. First, if that is you, I want to tell you that you are not at fault. Abusive behavior is *always* the responsibility of the abuser; there is nothing that you do that makes you *deserve* the abuse. Abuse is simply *never* okay. We always have choices about how we manage our anger. So no matter what your abuser says, you are not at fault.

And you are also not alone. Domestic violence is a very isolating experience. Isolation is a actually a very common tactic used by the abuser to keep their partner in the relationship; they know if you do not have support, do not have contact with friends, then you do not have options and you are dependent on your abuser—then it is very hard for you to leave the relationship. So it is very important for you to know that you are *not* alone and there is nothing shameful about the fact that someone else has chosen to hurt you or asking for help.

There is so much shame involved in being able to speak up about abuse. But you don't have to feel ashamed. There are many who have been abused and who have healed. There *are* options and there *is* hope. ::

That conversation with Ruth was a powerful moment for us at Good News. To be clear: there is no room, absolutely no place, zero tolerance, for abuse—not verbal, or psychological, or emotional, or financial, or sexual, or physical abuse—in the home, at work or school, in sports or in the church, in any of the relationships of followers of Jesus. No room for controlling, manipulating, belittling, threatening, intimidating behavior. (Some of you guys are big; and you intimidate others just by your size and presence, never mind your words; so you have to be aware of that dynamic and work extra hard to soften your presence.)

And if that abuse, if that controlling, intimidating behavior is happening, to any degree, at any level—in your home, in your dating relationship, in your marriage, with your children, with your aging parents, in your work relationships—you need to get help. If you are on the giving end, you need to get help. If you are on the receiving end, you need to get help. Talk with your pastor, talk with one of the elders or to their wives. Talk to a Christian counselor. Talk to your doctor. Talk to the police. But don't ignore it or deny it or minimize it or excuse it. *Get help.*

Getting a common misunderstanding right...

Unfortunately, in Christian circles, too often there's a misunderstanding of a few verses in Ephesians that some, who claim to be Christ-followers, hide behind. Look again at Ephesians, over one chapter, chapter 5, look down at verse 22. The apostle Paul writes, "Wives, submit to your husbands as to the Lord. For the husband is the head of the wife as Christ is the head of the church, his body, of which he is the Savior. Now as the church submits to Christ, so also wives should submit to their husbands in everything." Verse 25: "Husbands, love your wives, just as Christ loved the church and gave himself up for her to make her holy cleansing her by the washing with water through the word, and to present her to himself as a radiant church, without stain or wrinkle or any other blemish, but holy and blameless. In this same way, husbands ought to love their wives as their own bodies." Underline those verses, 22-28, in your bible.

There's a lot going on here that we can't talk about in this short book, but misunderstanding these verses is a major problem. Verse 22 again: "Wives, submit to your husbands..." Verse 24 "...wives should submit to their husbands in everything." Some guys take this idea of submission and they use it like a club: "The bible says I'm the boss here, I'm the head of this home! I'm the one who gives permission! You do what I want, what I say, or else there'll be consequences!"

Somehow in reading verse 22 these guys manage to skip over verse 21. Look back at Ephesians 4, verse 21 with me: "Submit to one another out of reverence for Christ." *What did that say?* "Submit to one another out of reverence for Christ." Louder? "Submit to one another out of reverence for Christ." Underline that verse too. Simple. Clear. No ambiguity. For disciples of Jesus, submission is mandatory and mutual. Women submit to men and men submit to women. There's no room for dominance, intimidation, control; no room for threats, coercion, violence. No. Mutual submission out of reverence for Christ. It's right there. Black and white.

Skip down to verse 25: Husbands, love your wives, (how?) just as Christ loved the church and gave himself up for her." How does this verse say that Christ loved the church? Sacrificially. He gave himself up for his bride, the church. That's how husbands are to love their wives. Not selfishly. Sacrificially. Humbly. Yet again Christ is our example. Putting your wife first. Before your job. Before your sports. Before your own comfort and convenience. Before yourself. Men are going to be held responsible, accountable by God, for how they handle this important and sacrificial role in the marriage relationship.

The key tool to communications in relationships...

Now I realize that not all abuse, not all control and manipulation, is men abusing or controlling women. Sometimes it's the other way around. What some women lack in size or voice-volume they make up for in controlling though withholding sex, or shrill nagging, through passive resistance and even violence. And sometimes the abuse is going both ways. So then how do you do what these verses say, how do you submit to each other? How do you sacrificially love each other?

Look back at Ephesians chapter 4, verse 29: "Do not let any unwholesome talk come out of your mouths, but only what is helpful for building others up according to their needs, that it may benefit those who listen. And do not grieve the Holy Spirit of God, with whom you were sealed for the day of redemption. Get rid of all bitterness, rage and anger, brawling and slander, along with every form of malice. (Instead) Be kind and compassionate to one another, forgiving each other, just as in Christ God forgave you!"

Underline those verses in your bible. Draw a box around them. Put an exclamation point next to them in the margin. This simple, short paragraph is the key biblical tool to healthy communication in relationships. I consider the principles found in this single, short verse to be the single most important tools in marriage counseling conversations. Let's take a moment and unpack those verses together...

First, "Do not let any unwholesome talk come out of your mouths..." What's that? Sure. You are in control of your emotions. Remember the telephone? *"Hel-lo!"* *"Do not let* any unwholesome talk come out of your mouth." You're in control of your emotions here. You choose your emotions. Learn to choose what you say with loving care.

Second, what's unwholesome? Well we know what unwholesome food is: it's spoiled, rotten, smells bad, tastes bad, it's not good for you. Same with unwholesome talk. Calling names. Cussing. I am shocked at how many people who say they are followers of Jesus are cussing and swearing like a Marine. Really? You say you're following Jesus? So does that mean you think Jesus talked like that?

> **Relationship counseling in one verse...**
>
> *Do not let any unwholesome talk come out of your mouths, but only what is helpful for building others up according to their needs, that it may benefit those who listen.*
>
> *- Ephesians 4:29*

Knock it off! No excuses. Remember the telephone! You choose your emotions. You choose your vocabulary. Your conversation at work, at home, on the sports field, in texting, in church should all be the same. If you can control your language at church, you can control it everywhere —it is simply a choice. And your choice reveals a lot.

Look at the rest of verse 29: "...but only what is helpful for building others up according to their needs, that it may benefit those who listen."

The 4 tests of healthy wholesome talk...

Look with me at these four tests here in verse 29 for figuring out good, wholesome, healthy talk. Test #1: Is it helpful? Is that cussing helpful? Really! What kind of talk is helpful in this conversation? Is that yelling helpful? Really!

Test #2: Only what is helpful for what? "...for building others up." The test is, "Does it build up?" Does my language, does my word choice, does my tone, does my body language, does that all work well for "building others up," for encouraging them, for coaching them to a win/win success in this situation? Or is my language tearing them down, beating them down, verbally whipping them, humiliating them, discouraging them, again?

Test #3: "Only what is helpful for building others up according to their needs."

The question to ask here is: What do they need right now? Become a student of your spouse. Study her. Learn about him. So what exactly can I say right now that will build her up according to her needs? Does she need simple kindness? Does she need some appreciation: "I love it when you do that!" "Thanks for doing that!" Does she need praise? "You look great when you wear those jeans!" Does he need affirmation? "I like it when you spend time with the grandkids." Does she need understanding: "Wow, looks like you've had a tough day; how about I take care of supper tonight while you take a bath?" Wives, what does your husband need right now? Understanding? "Are you afraid you might lose your job; is that why you're working all this overtime?" Praise? "Thanks for working so hard to support us..."

Test #4: "Do not let any unwholesome talk come out of your mouths, but only what is helpful for building others up according to their needs, that it may benefit those who listen." The question here is: What's the benefit? What's your goal here in this conversation? To win? To make him, or make her, do what you want? How about working to get to "...that it may *benefit* him, that it may benefit her?" What would build him up and encourage him and benefit him right now? How can I use this conversation to build her up and not tear her down?

> *The way to end the violence is to end the silence. Talk about abuse.*

Who wants a wife that has been torn down, beaten down, sworn at, discouraged, cowering, living in fear? I want Deb to be growing and happy and looking forward to it when I come home; not dreading it, not tip-toeing around trying to stay out of my way, not trying keep everything calm and smooth to avoid any possible blow ups. I want her to be happy. To love me and respect me, not fear me. Isn't that what you want, too?

So, how about you? I think we've kicked a few hornet's nests in this chapter. This anger thing, it's bad. But you don't have to live this way. It's a sin, just like my own battles with pride and wrestling with porn are sin. Your anger, your control issues, they're exactly what Jesus died on the cross for, so you can be forgiven and so you can be set free and empowered to live a life that's free of anger and its consequences. If any of this has struck close to home as you read this, see your pastor or one of the elders or their wives, and ask for help.

If you are a victim, please, talk to your pastor or his wife. Call a Christian counselor; send them an email or a text from your friend's phone if you have to. Or call the local crisis help line. But get some help. Don't live in fear any longer.

If this chapter didn't apply to you, but you know someone who's living in this every day, talk with them about it. The way to end the violence is to end the silence. Talk about abuse. Let's get beyond the cycles of anger and controlling behaviors. Let's set our kids up for success in their own relationships by fixing ours. Take a few minutes and pray about this.

Digging deeper...

1. Do you struggle with anger? What are the triggers in your life that always precipitate anger for you?

2. Now that you have identified the triggers, what tools can you put in place to help you control your anger?

3. What did you learn about Domestic Violence from Steve's interview with Ruth?

4. Do you know someone who is a victim of DV? Write out what you can do about that here...

5. Assignment: Write out Ephesians 4:29 on a card and memorize it.

CHAPTER 7

Supersized

Do you not know that your bodies are temples of the Holy Spirit, who is in you, whom you have received from God? You are not your own; you were bought at a price. Therefore honor God with your bodies.

- 1 Corinthians 6:19

I suspect that discussing the last of The Seven Deadly Sins on the classic list will make more than a few of us squirm and be quite uncomfortable. I know just studying for this chapter and reading the scriptures over was pretty uncomfortable, pretty convicting for me. So, whatever I say to you in the next few pages, just know that I'm saying it to myself first. And whatever the Holy Spirit is prompting in you in this chapter, I can tell you that I am hearing the Spirit speaking to me, too. Are you ready for this? Pause for a moment and pray before you read on.

So to start this conversation, turn in your bible with me to 1 Corinthians, chapter 6 and look down at verse 19 with me. The apostle Paul wrote "Do you not know that your bodies are temples of the Holy Spirit, who is in you, whom you have received from God? You are not your own; you were bought at a price. Therefore honor (or glorify) God with your bodies."

Simple truth and powerful gospel...

Underline those two verses in your bible. There's simple truth and powerful gospel (good news) here. First, the simple truth: all who believe in Jesus as the sinless Son of God who died on the cross for the forgiveness of their sins, who rose again to new life so that they can also be born again, all who are followers (or disciples) of Jesus have the Holy Spirit living inside them!

God doesn't live in magnificent cathedrals or simple chapels. This verse teaches us that you and I are the dwelling place, the temples, where the person of God the Holy Spirit lives. So when we say on Sunday morning that we acknowledge God's presence in our sanctuary, it's not as if some subtle spiritual mist or some gentle holy fog has come into the room. No, wherever God's people are, God is there, dwelling in, living in, his people.

The simple truth is that your body is a temple. You are the place where the Most High, the Holy Spirit of God dwells. And the powerful gospel in these verses is "You are not your own; you were bought at a price." What does that mean, "You are not your own; you were bought at a price?" The bible says that you and I were spiritually dead because of our sin (Ephesians 2:1; Colossians 2:13); damned and doomed on the broad highway to hell (Matthew 7:13, 14).

The bible describes us as lost, hopeless and helpless. "We all, like sheep, have gone astray, each of us has turned to our own way..." (Isaiah 53:6). "Remember that at that time you were separate from Christ without hope and without God in the world" (Ephesians 2:12).

But the good news of the gospel is that "At just the right time... (I love that!!) At just the right time, when we were still powerless, Christ died for the ungodly. Very rarely will anyone die for a righteous person, though for a good person someone might possibly dare to die. But God demonstrates his own love for us in this: While we were *still* sinners, Christ died for us!" (Romans 5:6-8).

Jesus died on the cross in my place to pay for my sin. Jesus died in *your* place to take on himself all of his Father's wrath for your sin. The price of my forgiveness—of your forgiveness—is nothing less than the horrible, violent, humiliating death of the sinless one, Jesus. I was bought—you were bought—with a price. A very high price. I don't want us to skip quickly past this powerful statement of the good news of the gospel.

If you are a believer in Jesus, God didn't send a good angel to take your punishment. And he didn't just say "Oh, that's okay. Really! No problem. Just forget about it!" No, the cost of your salvation, or your forgiveness, the cost of your redemption and justification in God's eyes was nothing less than the bloody death of Jesus (Ephesians 1:7; Matthew 26:28; 1 John 1:7), because the awesome holiness of God demands that sin be dealt with, not ignored (Hebrews 9:22). I don't know about you, but God's deep,

deep love for me and the very real cost of my salvation wrecks me every time I'm reminded by the bread and the cup of his body given for me, his blood that was shed for the forgiveness of all my sin. And it brings me to praise and worship.

So Paul writes "Do you not know that your bodies are temples of the Holy Spirit, who is in you, whom you have received from God? You are not your own; you were bought at a price. Therefore, honor God with your bodies."

You don't belong to you anymore...
Wow, no pressure! "You are not your own; you were bought at a price." You don't belong to you anymore! "You are not your own; you were bought at a price. Therefore, honor (or glorify) God with your bodies." Let that sink in for a moment. Soak in that for a moment. "You are not your own, you were bought with a price..."

This "honoring God with your body" thing has some serious implications for a whole pile of issues. Stop messing with drugs; illegal drugs, prescription drugs. Get help. Figure it out. "You are not your own; you were bought at a price. Therefore, honor God with your bodies." Stop drinking too much. Get help. "You are not your own; you were bought at a price. Therefore, honor God with your bodies." Stop killing yourself with smoking. "You are not your own; you were bought at a price. Therefore, honor God with your bodies." Stop sleeping with your girlfriend or boyfriend and marry her, marry him. "You are not your own; you were bought at a price. Therefore, honor God with your bodies."

And lose some weight. Number seven on our list of seven deadly sins is the little-talked-about but wildly popular sin of gluttony. And if you look around, at work, at school, on the street, I'm thinkin' we might have a problem with gluttony. Too much of a good thing. The statistics are ugly. Two thirds of adults are overweight or obese. Based on my Body Mass Index, I am obese. And according to the statistics, two out of every three adults in any room—and actually of the teens, too—are overweight or obese. More than 20% of all adolescents have weight-related diabetes or pre-diabetes; what doctors are calling the snowballing epidemic of *diabesity*.

Dr. Mehmet Oz writes that "There are 24 million diabetics in this country and about 6 million of them don't know it yet. The Centers for Disease Control estimate that one third of all Americans will develop diabetes and live 15 years less while losing measurable quality of life. It costs us $125 billion a year now to treat this killer and its complications and that cost is expected to double in the next 25 years."

Type 2 diabetes, the kind that usually comes from overeating, takes root when fat stored in the abdomen poisons the pancreas and causes it to stop producing insulin or the insulin in your blood cannot deliver glucose into your cells. Without insulin you cannot process sugar and without glucose your cells have no power supply.

Sugar is like glass...

Belly fat is a huge problem in America (pun intended). "The reason for the drastic increase is a perfect storm of poor diet and our sedentary lifestyle," writes Dr. Oz. "Why is diabetes so destructive? Quite simply in both Type 1 and Type 2 diabetes your body can't metabolize sugar, leaving it to float around in your bloodstream." But get this, Dr. Oz, a cardiothoracic surgeon and teaching professor at Columbia University, writes that "Sugar in your blood is like shards of glass scraping the inner lining of your arteries. The scrapes heal with *scar tissue* and cause blockages. The smaller blood vessels in your feet close completely and cut off circulation, requiring amputation as the tissue dies and becomes infected. The coronary arteries scar from the abuse by sugar shards in the blood and cause heart attacks and stroke. These sugar shards damage kidneys so severely they shrivel and die and patients often wind up on dialysis."

> **The Big Belly Test:**
>
> *Your waist should not measure (at your belly button) more than half your height*

Now here's the amazing good news: The symptoms are reversible! That's right. The symptoms of diabetes are reversible! Right now, according to the US Department of Agriculture (USDA), the average American eats 156 pounds of sugar per year, which is a little more than a five pound bag of sugar every two weeks! Sugar is hidden all kinds of places that you least expect—condiments such as salad dressing and ketchup, peanut butter, and of course juice and soda. "The intention of adding all this sugar wasn't to hurt anyone, it was just to get you to like their food. We've slipped into a cultural acceptance of 'a little sugar'—a little in our coffee, a little on our cereal, a lot in our soda, and it all adds up. The consequence of all that sweetness is obesity and rampant diabetes," writes Dr. Oz.

But back to the good news: 90 percent of diabetes is preventable and the symptoms are reversible. Let's go through a few risk factors and then some action steps: First, the warning signs of diabetes are constant thirst, frequency in urination, feeling tired, frequent infections, tingling in the toes, and vision problems. If you have any of these symptoms, see your doctor.

Second, the risk factors are a big belly which blocks insulin, a sedentary lifestyle, and a family history. When we talk about a "big belly" we mean one that measures more than half your height. If you are five foot 10 inches, (70 inches tall) your waist should measure no more than 35 inches at your belly button. So for me, that test means losing 6" around my middle or somehow growing to be 6'5"! Another rule of thumb is a woman of average height—5'4"-5'6"—should weigh less than 150 pounds for optimum health.

Can we change our genes or our biology? No. But we can nudge it in the right direction. How? Pretty simple, actually. Avoid/minimize the "white" foods: enriched flours, pasta, rice, and high-carbohydrate foods like potatoes, beets and carrots. Avoid high sugar soft drinks. Avoid high fructose corn syrup, which is found in everything from condiments to bread. Learn to read the label to see what's in a food item.

And exercise. There, I said it. You won't lose weight by exercising, but you will speed up your metabolism to help you burn calories, particularly if you are controlling sugar intake. Start by walking and set a goal to walk for 30 minutes, three times a week, then move gradually into an exercise program that your doctor approves.

Also, it is very helpful to know your numbers for BMI, blood sugar and blood pressure. Speak with your physician about your risk factors and get a screening. This is one of the most important decisions you can make for your health and your children's health. You owe it to yourself and your loved ones.

I'm not going to promote one diet over another. It's actually not about a diet. It's about changing the way you think about food. You can find some good tools to help you learn new ways to think about food, to eat, plan your

---

Major Diabetes Risk Factors

√ Family history of diabetes
√ Overweight (BMI ≥25)
√ Habitual physical inactivity
√ Race/ethnicity (e.g., African-Americans, Hispanic-Americans, Native Americans, Asian-Americans, & Pacific Islanders)
√ Hypertension (≥140/90)
√ HDL cholesterol ≤35 mg/dl and/or a triglyceride level ≥250
√ Delivery of a baby weighing >9#
√ Polycystic ovary syndrome

meals, get encouragement and support from other Christians online at helpful websites like Rick Warren's www.*DanielPlan.com* and Mike Copeland's www.*Setting CaptivesFree.com.*

When I finally began to come to terms with my weight in 2010, I realized I was only gaining, never losing weight. And I realized I was using food for comfort when I needed comfort. And I was using food for a reward when I was celebrating. As I thought about it, in just about any situation or occasion, food was the answer for me. Too much food. Food, in effect had become an idol in my life that too often took the place of God.

I've lost more than 20 pounds, with about 10 more to go—unless I suddenly grow to 6'5". I already feel better, sleep better, and I have more energy. I got off cholesterol and blood pressure meds. All good! But I couldn't do it without Deb. *USA Today* reported recently that more than half of us have tried to lose weight at one time or another. And many of us have tried multiple times. Success usually comes when you do it together with someone who can cheer for you, someone who can hold you accountable, someone who can walk, literally, beside you. That sounds a lot like a *Life Group* to me. Maybe your small group could take on a wellness project together, helping each other to lose some weight and build new habits for healthy eating and healthy living.

4 discipleship reasons why we are talking about fat...

So why is this pep talk on weight and our health choices part of a book on being a disciple of Jesus, replacing vices with virtues? I mean, what does "diabesity" or weight-loss have to do with being a follower of Jesus? Well, a lot more than you might think.

First, by the end of this decade, there will be 50 million people per year dying worldwide from life-style related diseases, compared to just (!) 20 million dying from infectious diseases. These are needless, premature deaths that can be prevented. And prevention has to start at home, with what you buy, what you order for takeout, what you order at Dunkin Donuts or Starbucks.

> *God made it.*
> *Jesus died for it.*
> *The Holy Spirit*
> *lives in it.*
> *Shouldn't you*
> *take care of it?*

The outrageous and immoral cost of this healthcare disaster is really all about stewardship. We have seen before that all we have, all we have been given, it all belongs to God, and we are his money managers, right? Psalm 24:1 says "The earth is the Lord's, and everything in it, the world, and all who live in it." But we're dropping the ball. It starts with the irresponsible immorality of spending God's money on all this sugar stuff that we know is harmful. Then there's spending more of God's money on the medications, the doctor's visits, the complications, the hospitalizations, the surgeries that our sugar-addiction have caused. So first, it's a moral issue because it's a stewardship issue.

Second, if you're anything like me, you might have let food become an idol that replaces God—that pushes God aside—for comfort, for pleasure, for reward. And idolatry is always wrong for a follower of Jesus. The apostle Paul talks about people whose god is their belly (Philippians 3:19). Gregory Beale said "We become what we worship, for ruin or restoration."[13] Jesus said it this way, "For where your treasure is, there your heart will be also" (Matthew 6:21). It is pretty obvious that way too many of us are worshipping our belly. Idolatry of food is a sin that needs to be confessed as sin. And like any sin we need to repent or turn away in a new direction.

Third, since God has placed you and me here for a purpose, since God chose you before the foundations of the world (Ephesians 1:4) and saved you and equipped/gifted you for his mission in the world (1 Corinthians 12:7; Ephesians 2:10; 4:12), then you matter, your part in the mission is important—it's important for yourself, for your family, and for advancing the kingdom mission of God. So you need to get your health under control or you won't be here to play your part. The writer of Hebrews tells us "Therefore, since we are surrounded by such a great cloud of witnesses, let us throw off everything (I think that includes overeating) that hinders and the sin that so easily entangles. And let us run with perseverance the race

---

[13] *We become What We Worship: A biblical Theology of Idolatry.* Gregory K. Beale. (Downers Grove: IVP Academic, 2008).

marked out for us, fixing our eyes on Jesus, the pioneer and perfecter of faith" (Hebrews 12:1, 2).

Take care of the temple...

Fourth, we just saw in 1 Corinthians 6 that your body is the temple of God. "Do you not know that your bodies are temples of the Holy Spirit, who is in you, whom you have received from God? You are not your own; you were bought at a price. Therefore honor God with your bodies." Here's the thing, summarized in Rick Warren's simple, concise statement: "God made it. Jesus died for it. The Holy Spirit lives in it. Shouldn't you take care of it?" Take a moment and consider what God is saying to you in this chapter.

Digging deeper...

1. 1 Corinthians 6:19: "Do you not know that your bodies are temples of the Holy Spirit, who is in you, whom you have received from God? You are not your own; you were bought at a price. Therefore honor God with your bodies." What is the Simple Truth in this verse? Write your answer here, and what that means for you...

2. What is the Powerful Gospel? (pp. 93, 94) Write your answer here, and what that means for you...

3. How did you make out with the Big Belly Test?(p. 97) What are you going to do about it? Write it out.

4. Steve gave four "discipleship reasons" (pp. 100-103) why Gluttony is a spiritual issue. Do any of them apply to you? Explain here...

5. Quoting Rick Warren, Steve wrote "God made it. Jesus died for it. The Holy Spirit lives in it. Shouldn't you take care of it?" Explain what that means for you by answering two questions: What do you think? What will you do?

6. Assignment: Write out 1 Corinthians 6:19 on a card and memorize it.

CHAPTER 8

P-E-G-L-A-G-S

Therefore do not let sin reign in your mortal body so that you obey its evil desires. Do not offer any part of yourself to sin as an instrument of wickedness, but rather offer yourselves to God as those who have been brought from death to life; and offer every part of yourself to him as an instrument of righteousness. - Romans 6:12, 13

Since we have these promises, dear friends, let us purify ourselves from everything that contaminates body and spirit, perfecting holiness out of reverence for God.
- 2 Corinthians 7:1

One way to remember the classic list of The Seven Deadly Sins is to use the simple mnemonic device, PEGLAGS, which stands for Pride, Envy, Greed, Lust, Anger, Gluttony and Sloth.

What is important is the realization that all of these seven deadly sins—actually, all sinful behavior—begins in the desires in our mind. It begins with a thought, a temptation. And that thought, when given our permission—the freedom to develop into action—becomes sin. Look at James 1:13-15: "When tempted, no one should say, 'God is tempting me.' For God cannot be tempted by evil, nor does he tempt anyone; but each one is tempted when, by his own evil desire, he is dragged away and enticed. Then, after desire has conceived, it gives birth to sin; and sin, when it is full-grown, gives birth to death."

Bob Gilbert shared this diagram with me that is quite insightful and helpful:

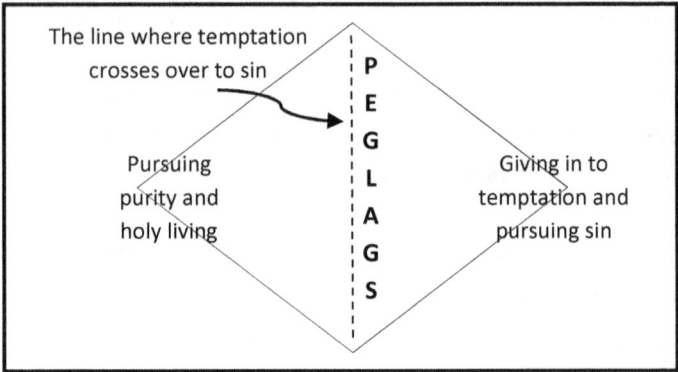

Controlling our thought life...

There is a line where temptation crosses over to sin. So we have a choice. First, we know the temptation itself is not sinful. We know that Jesus "...was tempted in every way as we are, yet without sin" (Hebrews 4:15). If Jesus was tempted, but did not sin, then the temptation itself is not sinful. For example, there is a difference between having sexual feelings, as we all do, and letting them grow into lustful thoughts which we then act on. When Martin Luther was talking about impure thoughts, he said, "You can't stop the birds from flying over your head, but you can keep them from building a nest in your hair."

Jerry Bridges, in his classic best-seller *The Pursuit of Holiness*, writes "We may determine by God's grace to stop a sinful habit—entertaining lustful thoughts, criticizing a Christian brother, or whatever. But alas, only too frequently we do not succeed." He goes on: "Paul says that we are to train or discipline ourselves to be godly. The figure of speech he uses comes from the disciplined and rigorous physical training that Greek Olympic athletes went through. 'Everyone who competes in the games goes into strict training.' (1 Corinthians 9:25). He said this is the attitude of life that a Christian should have." It is pretty obvious that resisting temptation will not come easily or naturally.[14]

Take every thought captive

It is essential to carefully control what we allow ourselves to see, hear, read, and experience.

What are the disciplines that we need to practice to resist temptation? Keeping the pesky birds away—

---

[14] Speaking of resisting, make sure you resist the temptation to judge others who are struggling with sin, particularly with sins you are not tempted to indulge in. Start by cultivating a humble heart. Billy Graham said, "Never take credit for not falling into a temptation that never tempted you in the first place."

successfully resisting the temptation to pride, envy, greed, lust, anger, gluttony and sloth—begins first with the apostle Paul's inspired advice to "Take every thought captive to make it obedient to Christ" (2 Corinthians 10:5).

Thoughts are both simple and complex things. Here. Gone. Coming back. Never remembered. But out of our thoughts comes our view of ourselves, our view of our world, and the actions (and reactions) of our daily life; actions which, when repeated just a few times, quickly become the habits of a lifetime.

So Paul rightly urges us to "Take every thought captive..." It is essential to carefully control what we allow ourselves to see, hear, read, and experience. My wife Deb likes to use the old 1960s acronym, GI-GO, for "Garbage in—Garbage Out." Some fleeting images burn their impression deeply. And innocence once lost is lost forever. So first, take every thought captive. Discipline yourself to control what you consume in your mind.

> *"I have stored up Your word in my heart that I might not sin against You"*
>
> Psalm 119:11

Hide God's Word in your heart...

Second, hide God's word in your heart. Over the years I have realized that this simple tool is critical to successfully resisting temptation. It's what David, the "man after God's own heart," had to do. He wrote "I have stored up your word in my heart that I might not sin against you" (Psalm119:11). Many different scriptures coach us, instruct us, urge us to saturate our minds with the powerful truths and principles of the Word of God. Here's just a few: God said "These commandments that I give you today are to be upon your hearts" (Deuteronomy 6:6). The Psalm-writer said "Direct my footsteps according to your word; let no sin rule over me" (Psalm 119:133). And again, "Seven times a day I praise you for your righteous rules. Great peace have they who love your law, and nothing can make them stumble" (Psalm 119:164, 165).

> **The 5 steps of bible memory:**
>
> *Write it out.*
> *Read it over.*
> *Say it over.*
> *Repeat it.*
> *Use it in prayer.*

And over the years I have found peace and counsel, clarity, direction and comfort at just the right moment with the sudden recall of truths and promises of God's word that have been memorized, usually when I was a child. I have also discovered that unfortunately it is not quite as easy to memorize Scripture now as it was when I was a kid. The younger the better. But the five simple steps of bible memory remain the same. Write it out by hand (which involves multiples sensory inputs to your brain) on a card that you can carry with you. Read it over. Say it over out loud. Repeat it multiple times throughout the day. Use it in your prayer. See the Appendix for a great list of foundational verses that will begin to shape your mind for Christ-likeness.

We need to fill our minds with the deep truths of Scripture because our culture is utilizing the latest incredible technology and spending billions of dollars and untold hours to fill our minds with lies. "Lust is okay, you're only human." "Greed is good!" "Supersize that fast-food order and you'll save money." "It's her fault that I got angry." "The one who dies with the most toys wins!" "You need a bigger flat screen TV to enjoy the R-rated movies in your premium HD cable package." "A little porn doesn't hurt anyone. And it satisfies your desires." And on the lies go.

The only way to push the lies out of your mind is to saturate your mind with the truth. Deep truth. Truth found in God's word. Ultimately, if you are going to have victory over the temptation of the seven deadly sins, it will be a spiritual victory first—a victory in your mind, a mind that is captivated by the joy of loving God and pleasing God, a mind that is enthralled with praising and worshipping God, a mind that is overwhelmed with God's love, grace and mercy, a mind that is saturated, soaked, drenched with God's truth.

> *"You will keep him in perfect peace*
> *whose mind is stayed on you."*
> - Isaiah 26:3

Digging deeper...

1. After exploring PEGLAGS together (p. 105), what has the Holy Spirit been speaking about to the inner you that you have had to confront in this study?

2. Can you see where the line is between facing temptation and surrendering to temptation (p. 106)? What do you need to do to protect yourself from crossing that line?

3. The Apostle Paul wrote "Take every thought captive to make it obedient to Christ" (2 Corinthians 10:5). What does that mean for you; how can you "Take every thought captive?"

4. King David wrote, "I have stored up your word in my heart that I might not sin against you" (Psalm119:11). How can memorization of scripture help you to confront the seven deadly sins? What is your plan?

The Navigators Topical Memory System

If you want to memorize Scripture, but aren't sure where to begin, or what to memorize, this simple list used for decades by The Navigators (navigators.org/us/resources) is exactly what you need to begin hiding God's word in your heart.

LIVE THE NEW LIFE IN CHRIST

Christ the Center	2 Corinthians 5:17	Galatians 2:20
Obedience to Christ	Romans 12:1	John 14:21
The Word	2 Timothy 3:16	Joshua 1:8
Prayer	John 15:7	Phil. 4:6, 7
Fellowship	Matthew 18:20	Heb 10:24, 25
Witnessing	Matthew 4:19	Romans 1:16

PROCLAIM CHRIST

All Have Sinned	Romans 3:23	Isaiah 53:6
Sin's Penalty	Romans 6:23	Hebrews 9:27
Christ Paid the Penalty	Romans 5:8	1 Pt 3:18
Must Receive Christ	John 1:12	Revelation 3:20
Assurance of Salvation	1 John 5:13	John 5:24
Salvation is not by Works	Ephesians 2:8, 9	Titus 3:5

RELY ON GOD'S RESOURCES

His Spirit	1 Corinthians 3:16	1 Cor 2:12
His Strength	Isaiah 41:10	Philippians 4:13
His Faithfulness	Lamentations 3:22, 23	Numbers 23:19
His Peace	Isaiah 26:3	1 Peter 5:7
His Provision	Romans 8:32	Philippians 4:19
His help in Temptation	Hebrews 2:18	Ps. 119:9, 11

BE CHRIST'S DISCIPLE

Put Christ First	Matthew 6:33	Luke 9:23
Be Steadfast	1 Corinthians 15:58	Hebrews 12:3
Serve Others	Mark 10:45	2 Cor. 4:5
Give Generously	Proverbs 3:9, 10	2 Cor. 9:6,7
Separate from the World	1 John 2:15, 16	Romans 12:2

GROW IN CHRISTLIKENESS

Love	John 13:34, 35	1 John 3:18
Humility	Philippians 2:3, 4	1 Peter 5:5,6
Purity	Ephesians 5:3	1 Peter 2:11
Honesty	Leviticus 19:11	Acts 24:16
Faith	Hebrews 11:6	Romans 4:20,21
Good Works	Galatians 6:9, 10	Matthew 5:16

About the author

Steve grew up in a small town in Rhode Island. After working in the marketplace for 25 years in an advertising agency he was asked in 2005 to serve as the teaching pastor at Good News Bible Chapel in Attleboro, Massachusetts (USA) where his family had been serving for decades, and he had been serving as an elder.

Steve's primary ministry at the Chapel is in preaching and making disciples, teaching the body of Christ by example how to get outside the walls of the Chapel and unite with "the church of Attleboro" to love the city of Attleboro in simple, practical and generous ways. He is a co-founder of *The Saltshaker* in Attleboro, a multi-fellowship, cross-denominational ministry of compassion and evangelism.

Steve and his wife Deb have three married kids and seven grandchildren (to date). They enjoy kayaking the rivers of New England, quiet late night suppers, and getting lots of family time.

Steve was educated at Rhode Island College, Trinity International University (TEDS), and is a *summa cum laude* graduate of Gordon-Conwell Theological Seminary (MA – Urban Ministry).

Also by Steve DuPlessie...

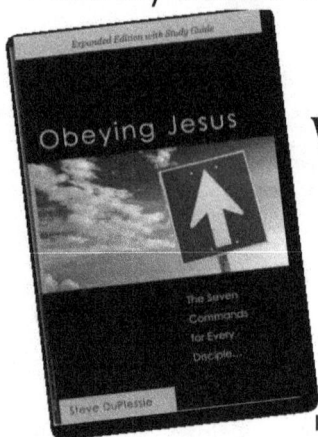

What does being a disciple of Jesus look like?

In his last moments on earth with his core disciples, Jesus said "Go and make disciples ... teaching them to obey all that I have commanded." So, what are these commands that sincere, authentic followers of Jesus should be obeying?

In *Obeying Jesus*, Steve DuPlessie outlines the seven critical commands for every Christ-follower—with some important warnings, some very practical suggestions, and a built-in Study Guide for individuals and groups.

Encouraging for new believers, useful for those in the trenches of making disciples, and challenging for mature believers, *Obeying Jesus* offers a positive, helpful focus on what it means to make and be a disciple in the 21st century.

"Your book is delightful, refreshing, and focused on the essentials. I particularly like your 'Danger Danger Danger!' chapter."
— **George Patterson**, veteran missionary to Honduras, church planter, *Western Seminary* professor, and founder of the church planting network *People of Yes!*

"In Obeying Jesus *Steve has forever changed my understanding and application of Jesus' final charge to those who would follow him."*
— **Dr. Bruce Hanlon,** Professor of Theology, *African Bible College*, Malawi

"This book can not only help you grow more like Jesus, it can help you help others too."
— **Dennis Fuqua**, President, *International Renewal Ministries,* Vancouver, Washington. Author of *Living Prayer: The Lord's Prayer Alive in You and United and Ignited: Encountering God through Dynamic Corporate Prayer*

Available in paper and e-reader at amazon.com